STRATEGIC ANALYSIS

AND ACTION

FOURTH EDITION

JOSEPH N. FRY
Richard Ivey School of Business
The University of Western Ontario

J. PETER KILLING
International Institute for Management Development

PRENTICE HALL CANADA INC., SCARBOROUGH, ONTARIO

Canadian Cataloguing in Publication Data

Fry, Joseph N., 1936–
       Strategic analysis and action

4th ed.
ISBN 0-13-020932-5

1. Business planning. 2. Strategic planning. I. Killing, J. Peter.
II. Title.

HD31.F79 2000   658.4′012   C98-932932-1

Prentice-Hall, Inc., Upper Saddle River, New Jersey
Prentice-Hall International (UK) Limited, London
Prentice-Hall of Australia, Pty. Limited, Sydney
Prentice-Hall Hispanoamericana, S.A., Mexico City
Prentice-Hall of India Private Limited, New Delhi
Prentice-Hall of Japan, Inc., Tokyo
Simon & Schuster Southeast Asia Private Limited, Singapore
Editora Prentice-Hall do Brasil, Ltda., Rio de Janeiro

ISBN 0-13-020932-5

Publisher: Patrick Ferrier
Acquisitions Editor: Mike Ryan
Associate Editor: Sherry Torchinsky
Senior Marketing Manager: Ann Byford
Production Editor: Nicole Mellow
Copy Editor: Ann McInnis
Production Coordinator: Jane Schell
Art Director: Mary Opper
Cover Design: Carole Knox
Cover Image: Phototone
Interior Design: Sarah Battersby
Page Layout: Heidi Palfrey

1 2 3 4 5   04 03 02 01 00

Printed and bound in Canada

Visit the Prentice Hall Canada Web site! Send us your comments,
browse our catalogues, and more at **www.phcanada.com**.
Or reach us through e-mail at **phcinfo_pubcanada@prenhall.com**.

To our wives, Cherie Lind and Rebecca

CONTENTS

PREFACE

This book was written to complement case analysis in university and company strategic management courses. It takes the point of view of the general manager and presents a consistent, operational approach to analyzing and acting on strategic problems.

As we point out in Chapter 1, general managers run businesses, and, while their responsibility may be for a small business or a large corporation, they face the common challenge of guiding their organizations to success in a competitive environment. The aim of this book is to develop the basic general management skills required to understand a business, sense the opportunities and problems that it faces, deal effectively with strategic decisions, and set in place the people and operations to implement those decisions.

In preparing the text materials, we have concentrated on analytic concepts that contribute to a practical understanding of specific strategic issues and to the translation of this understanding into personal action. Further, we have linked these discrete concepts into a comprehensive framework—the Diamond-E framework—to ensure that the whole of the situation facing the business is appreciated and that priorities are set for both analysis and action.

We have made two assumptions about our readers. First, we have assumed that they are engaged in trying to solve strategic problems—as students doing case analyses or field projects, or as managers on the job. Application and practice are the prime vehicles for understanding the power and limitations of the concepts in this text and, more importantly, for developing general management skills. Second, we have assumed that our readers possess a basic understanding of the background disciplines and functional areas of business, such as the financial analysis and marketing skills provided in early courses in university business programs.

This is a textbook. Its contribution lies in the originality of its purpose and presentation. As we prepared the materials, we drew on the work of specialized researchers and writers in strategic management and associated fields. Specific contributions are cited, but we would also like to acknowledge our general debt to those who have been part of building a better understanding of management practice.

The first edition of this book was published in 1986. In revising it for this fourth edition, we have relied on our subsequent teaching and consulting experience to sharpen important points and to explain procedures more effectively. We have continued our efforts to make the text increasingly user friendly by clarifying the terminology of the basic frameworks, by putting more emphasis on the processes for putting these frameworks to work, and by expanding the use of examples. Throughout, our aim has been to increase the relevance of the materials for solving general management problems in the field or in the form of written cases. The entire text is closely aligned with a new companion casebook, *Strategic Management: A Canadian Casebook,* Fifth Edition.

We have been fortunate to work for many years in institutions that value good teaching and professional relevance. These cultural attributes have been developed and reinforced by many people. In all editions we have benefited from the new ideas and continuing support of our colleagues in the university and in the private sector. We would particularly like to acknowledge our immediate colleagues at the Richard Ivey School of Business and at IMD who, over the years, have included professors Paul Beamish, the late Harold Crookell, Mary Crossan, Jim Dowd, Michael Geringer, Gerald Higgins, Mike Levenhagen, Alan Morrison, Tom Poynter, Paul Strebel, Don Thain, Bart Victor, and Rod White.

Joseph N. Fry
London, Ontario

J. Peter Killing
Lausanne, Switzerland

INTRODUCTION

This introduction is your owner's manual. It explains the approach and organization of the book and suggests how you can best use it.

Approach

The book was prepared as a practical guide for strategic analysis and action. We have designed it for readers who are working on applied strategic problems, either through case studies or on-the-job assignments. It provides an organized set of concepts and procedures to help readers identify strategic issues, make choices, and implement decisions.

The point of view we take on strategic issues is that of a general manager. We assume that you are willing to share this perspective—to see yourself as responsible for the overall direction and success of a business unit. First, you must think in comprehensive terms of the total problem you are dealing with, taking into account the full breadth of its meaning and consequences for the business. Partial analyses from a specialist or a functional perspective may be helpful, but they do not meet the general manager's need for the best overall approach to a situation. In addition to the broad issues of direction, you must worry about the specific steps of implementation—about closing the gaps between strategic choice and practical, personal action. Again, the recommendations of a consultant or staff specialist may be useful, but this advice will usually address only the directional aspects of the general manager's concerns. In short, we ask you to step into a particularly challenging position in which you must think of problems in terms of a total business, set priorities, and plan for tangible, practical action.

The choice and presentation of material in the book have been guided by practical utility. Our aim has been to provide useful tools organized into one consistent and comprehensive framework. We have drawn heavily on the available literature in developing this approach, but we have deliberately avoided detailed reviews and discussions in the text of alternative definitions, concepts, and procedures. Additional readings are suggested, where appropriate, at the end of chapters for those who wish to explore specific subjects in greater depth.

Throughout the book, we have frequently used examples to make the connection between the concepts, which have to be somewhat general for flexibility and breadth of application, and specific strategic issues. As you read, you might find it useful to think of examples from your own experience and test the applicability of the concepts against them.

Organization

The book is organized according to a general pattern: problem identification to decision to implementation. This is a natural, logical sequence and is effective for the cumulative presentation of concepts. But we do not mean to imply that actual strategic problems can be dealt with in such a neat, serial fashion. On the contrary, most strategic problems require an iterative approach, in which the analysis moves back and forth between choice and action. This point will become evident as you read through the book. Its immediate application, however, is that you should not expect to find business situations, or case problems describing them, that neatly conform to the flow of the text.

There are 10 chapters in the book. Chapters 1 and 2 position the concept of strategy as a crucial general management tool and then provide an operational understanding and definition of it. Chapter 3 introduces the Diamond-E framework and the fundamental logic of strategic analysis. Chapters 4 through 7 elaborate on the processes of analysis by working through the individual components of the Diamond-E framework with a view to building a comprehensive position on strategic needs and priorities. Chapter 8 provides a transition to specific issues of implementation that leads to Chapters 9 and 10, which concentrate on developing personal action plans to move from the analytic results to the implementation of strategic changes.

Suggestions for Use

At the outset we suggest that you read Chapters 1 through 3 thoroughly. This will provide a perspective for your thinking and a basic framework for your analysis. Skim the rest of the book so that you know where to turn as specific circumstances dictate.

As you deal with problems, use the book selectively. Try to work back and forth between the problem that you are addressing and the relevant parts of the book. Use the concepts to check your analysis and, as necessary, to expand it. Common sense is very important here. Don't try to force the concepts and procedures on a problem; instead use them to enrich the analysis.

Study the book after you have spent some time working on strategic problems. At that point you will more readily appreciate the general analytical approach and see the applicability of particular concepts. From then on, the building of skills in strategic analysis and action is a matter of practice and more practice. Remember, you are dealing with the most complex problems in business. Good luck!

THE JOB OF THE GENERAL MANAGER

General managers run businesses. Although their assignments may vary widely, from that of chief executive of a global company to the manager of a profit centre inside the firm, general managers are all faced with the task of guiding their business to success in a rapidly changing competitive environment. As the millennium dawns, this is not getting any easier.

THE CHALLENGE

The fundamental challenge facing general managers today stems from the fact that the external environment in which their firm operates—current customers, potential customers, competitors, regulators, suppliers, and so on—is changing so rapidly that the firm, with its finite resources and limited organizational capabilities, is hard-pressed to keep up. And keep up it must, because in a rapidly changing environment, sticking with yesterday's strategy, no matter how successful it has been, is often a recipe for tomorrow's disaster.

Until very recently, many global companies assumed that their growth for at least the next decade would be in Asia. Western markets were mature, and the quickly growing economies of countries such as Thailand, Vietnam, Indonesia, Korea, and, above all, China would be "where the action is." Now Asia has collapsed, China is very difficult, and India may not be as open to foreigners as was previously hoped. What assumptions should a manager make about the future of these markets? What should today's strategy be, given such uncertainty? Attack? Retreat? Wait and see?

Massive changes are also taking place on the competitive front. One need look no further than the airline, financial services, or pharmaceutical industries to see former competitors either buying one another, or becoming alliance partners at an unprecedented rate. In industry after industry there is a feeling that global consolidation is under way, and that only a few massive firms will be left standing at the end. Whether this is in fact correct, no one knows, but acquisitions like that of Chrysler by Daimler-Benz send shock waves through an industry. Who will be next? Can any major player afford to remain alone? Is now the time to buy a much-weakened Korean competitor?

A second area of major challenge is inside the firm. It is clear that the organization needs to develop new capabilities to allow the effective implementation of new strategies, and in less time than ever before. But how should this be done? How will your organization need to function in five years' time? The cost of communication is falling dramatically, and some general managers receive and send hundreds of E-mails every day. Is this a waste of the CEO's time, or is it a fundamental source of competitive advantage? And what about creating a flatter organization structure, and "empowering" managers and frontline workers? Are these key elements in the race to build new capabilities, or fads that will soon be replaced by something else? The challenges are clearer than the solutions, and the thoughtful general manager needs to make decisions that are right for his or her organization, and not indiscriminately adopt the latest "hot idea."

THE JOB OF THE GENERAL MANAGER

Turbulent external environments give rise to a continuing stream of opportunities as well as challenges. Put most simply, the job of the general manager is to ensure that the organization is able to capitalize on the most appropriate opportunities, while meeting or avoiding the challenges to its existing business. As a general manager you need to recognize emerging opportunities and challenges, prepare a response, and ensure the success of whatever plan of action you decide upon. By way of example, consider the rapidly changing competitive situation in the international courier services industry.

The first major move by an "outsider" into the courier business was in 1996 when KPN, the privatized Dutch post office, bought TNT, a major international courier service based in Australia. Then in 1998, Deutsche Post, the German post office, acquired 22 percent of DHL International. These were significant strategic moves for these two post offices, taking them well beyond their traditional sphere of operation. What challenges and opportunities drove the general managers in these national post offices to make these moves? The challenges, one suspects, were coming from the rise of fax, E-mail, and courier services, and a concurrent decline in the price of telephone calls. The opportunity, on the other hand, was to combine the international delivery systems developed by the couriers with the individual postal stations and door-to-door networks of the post offices. Deutsche Post, for example, planned to market DHL's air-based overnight delivery service through its 15 000 postal stations.

Are these national post offices making the right moves? Only the future will tell, but one thing is clear: there are many more national post offices than there are major international courier services and not everyone is going to be able to adopt this strategy. Those making the first moves might be the winners, but these acquisitions could end up being a cautionary tale for others in the industry of a route *not* to follow.

Fundamental strategic decisions like these will affect a business for years, and are best made when senior managers have a clear sense of the organization's long-term direction. A newly privatized post office, for example, needs to develop a mission that elaborates its new long-term purpose, and a vision that addresses issues such as how quickly (if at all) it wants to grow outside its domestic market, and to what extent it will move beyond its traditional postal stations and door-to-door delivery services. These determinations need to take into account things like the probable impact of the Internet (many goods sold over the Internet will need to be physically delivered to individual homes); the entry of new competitors into the home market, which for most post offices was previously a monopoly; the use of Internet advertising to replace direct mail; and so on.

Having established a long-term direction, and made a major strategic move, the general manager's work is not done. In fact, the most difficult part is just beginning. To make these new investments succeed, KPN and Deutsche Post executives needed to decide to what extent, and how, to integrate their courier operations, to maximize the capability of the combined organization. Clearly, bringing together employees with the conservative attitudes and behaviours gained from working in a long-established monopolist post office, with those of a much younger, international, highly competitive, fast-growing courier service (DHL International had been growing at 20–25 percent annual rate immediately prior to the Deutsche Post investment) will require considerable thought and care. Changes in attitude and ways of working will probably be required on both sides.

This example illustrates three of the fundamental components of the general manager's job: setting direction, creating strategy, and implementing change. There is one further crucial aspect of the job, shown in Figure 1.1: assessing performance—both current and longer term. Without a good feel for how well the organization is performing at any point in time, a general manager could get the other three components of the job very wrong. Emphasizing lofty but distant goals when the company may not survive the coming year could lead to disaster; acting as if there is a crisis when a slower pace of change would be more appropriate can be just as damaging. KPN and Deutsche Post were vulnerable, as their protected domestic markets were opened to competition; they may well have seen a performance decline ahead, and from this came their preparedness to strike out in a new and risky, but potentially rewarding, direction.

3

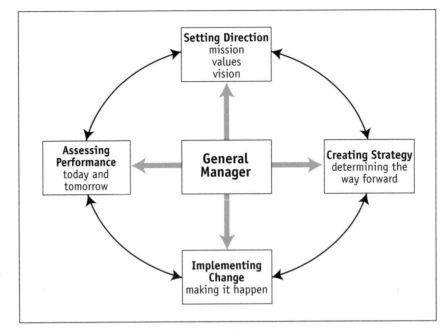

FIGURE 1.1
**The Job of
the General
Manager**

A competent general manager will perform all four of these tasks. These will not be addressed sequentially or in isolation from each other, but as a continuously changing mix of activities. The double-headed arrows in Figure 1.1 are intended to convey this interconnectedness.

The primary focus of this book is on the processes and tools that you will need for creating strategy and managing change. But before you embark on the strategy-making process you need to make sure that you know where you are starting from, which means that you need a solid assessment of today's performance. You also need a high-level view of what you are trying to achieve. This is most likely captured in your mission, values, and vision. In the remainder of this chapter we shall address these topics.

ASSESSING PERFORMANCE

We begin with a discussion of performance assessment because the general manager who is not good at this will have great difficulty with the other aspects of the job. Many corporate tragedies are rooted in the fact that senior managers had a false idea of how well their organization was performing. Managers in Xerox for years underestimated the threat of Japanese competition in the copier business because they did not pay attention to the share that relatively slow and inexpensive copiers were taking of the total market. Xerox eventually saw the need to change, but it was very, very late.

TABLE 1.1
Typical Measures of Operating Performance

Profitability	Financial Position	Market Performance
• profit margins (gross and operating)	• leverage ratios (debt/equity, interest coverage)	• absolute level and growth rate in sales
• key expense ratios	• liquidity ratios (units, revenue)	• market share
• return on equity, assets	• activity ratios (e.g., asset and inventory turnover)	• new products as % of sales
• economic value added		

Our assessment of organizational performance is based on two sets of measures: *operating performance* and *organizational health*. Some typical measures of operating performance are included in Table 1.1. In any given situation some of these measures may be more important than others. Whatever your circumstances, beware of relying on only a single measure of operating performance, or on solely internal measures. Consider, for example, that changes in market performance generally precede changes in financial performance, and can provide an early indication that something is wrong. This may occur if customers who are not happy with the quality of your product cannot change to a competitor's product until they use up their existing inventory or modify their process to accept the competing product. Thus, customer satisfaction may well decline before you see any change in market share. Even when share does fall at the consumer level, it may not show up in your financial results immediately if a distributor stocks your product. Clearly, multiple measures of operating performance are very useful.[1]

Measures of organizational health are generally "softer" than those of operating performance, and include such things as management and worker enthusiasm for what they are doing, the ability to work across boundaries, and the ability of the organization to learn. These and other factors are described in Table 1.2. Again, you might put more emphasis on some of these factors than others as you are assessing the health of your organization, but again we recommend that you focus on more than a single measure, and assess how these factors are changing over time.

The danger that many senior management teams face is that they think they know where the business stands in terms of organizational health, but in fact they do not. This could be because negative communication to the top of

TABLE 1.2
Typical Measures of Organizational Health

Enthusiasm	Boundaries	Problem Solving	Learning	Sustainability
How enthusiastic are managers and employees about their work?	Do individuals identify with narrow sub-groups, or with the organization as a whole?	Are problem areas identified and dealt with, or hidden and ignored?	Does the organization learn from its experiences? From others' experiences?	Can the pace at which people are working be sustained?

Source: Adapted from R. Pascale, M. Millimann, and L. Gioja, "Changing the Way We Change," *Harvard Business Review,* (November–December 1997).

the organization is implicitly or explicitly discouraged, it could be the result of middle managers choosing to filter information before it reaches the top, or simply that senior managers do not listen well. One response in many firms has been to use anonymous employee surveys on a large scale to try to get a realistic assessment of these measures.

Using the Performance Matrix

We use the performance matrix to classify operating performance and organizational health as roughly positive or negative and ask three questions: (1) where was your business three years ago? (2) where is it today? and (3) which way is it currently moving? Our main emphasis is on the current position of the business, but a discussion of this naturally leads to consideration of where the business has been and which way it is moving.

In Figure 1.2 we have illustrated the hypothetical case of a business that has moved from Quadrant 2 (Q2) through Q4 and is currently in Q3, hoping to move upward to Q1. This has not been an unusual path in the 1990s, and we thought it worth explaining a little further what it means to place your business in each of these quadrants.

Clearly, the desired state is Quadrant 1, in which operating performance and organizational health are both positive. If your analysis suggests that your business is in this quadrant, and you expect it to stay there, your strategy review will probably be a question of fine tuning, and perhaps taking a farther than usual look into the future. But do not take the strategy assessment process lightly. You need to ensure that you have placed yourself in this quadrant as a result of thorough analysis, not complacency or wishful thinking.

The picture in Quadrant 2, on the other hand, may be of an inward-looking and complacent organization where people enjoy their work, but collectively are performing inadequately in terms of market and financial standards. There may be recognition by a few that there is a need to change, but getting a meaningful strategic review under way may be difficult, as currently happy employees will not want to face the prospect of making uncomfortable changes to improve operating performance.

In Quadrant 3 the business is achieving its operating objectives at the expense of organizational health. This is a common situation at the end of the 1990s, in businesses where management has applied pressure for short-term profits, often via downsizing, without upgrading the skills of their people, and giving little thought to the processes by which work should be done. It is a classic case of doing the same work with fewer people, and everyone is burned out.

Quadrant 4 represents a clear-cut problem situation in which immediate and comprehensive action is necessary. It may well be a crisis; if so, strategic analysis had better be fast. Shortcuts may have to be taken, but our hope is that a quick look through this book will at least help you decide where to start, and which parts of the strategy creation process will yield the most value to you and your business team.

In later chapters we will discuss other perspectives on performance. In Chapter 4, for example, we will ask you to predict the likely performance of your business if it continues with its existing strategy; this is your "base case" scenario. In the last two chapters of the book, which deal with the management of change, we will discuss the crisis curve concept, which involves tracing the past, current, and projected future performance of a business, to determine the urgency for change.

We now turn to another task of the general manager that needs to be considered before we turn to strategy: that of establishing the overall direction for the business.

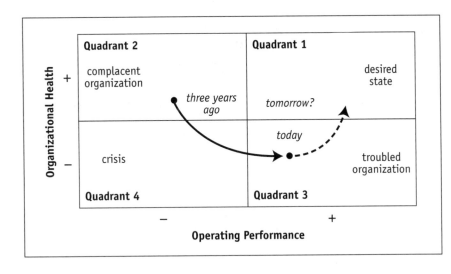

FIGURE 1.2

The Performance Matrix (with illustrative example)

SETTING DIRECTION: MISSION, VALUES, VISION

Organizations need a strong sense of direction to bring coherence to the many strategic and operating decisions that managers at all levels are constantly called upon to make. In response, many have developed mission statements, declarations of corporate values, and vision statements. Such statements usually indicate in a general sense where the business is going, and how it is to be managed.

Unfortunately the words *mission, values,* and *vision* are often used with a variety of inconsistent meanings in casual business conversation and even in formal documents. Our approach, therefore, has been to develop and work with one clear set of definitions that are consistent within themselves, and with common usage to the extent that this was possible.

We use mission, values, and vision to refer to elements of belief or corporate intent that are likely to be of longer duration than the current strategy (the elements of which will be described in Chapter 2). For 20 years, Komatsu, the small Japanese company that grew to become the second-largest earth moving equipment company in the world, had a simple but motivating mission: to "beat Caterpillar," the world leader. The 3M company has had a central value of fostering individual entrepreneurship since the early 1900s. And it was outstanding individual efforts that brought the company Scotch tape, Thinsulate, Post-it notes, and a variety of other highly successful products, decade after decade.

We differentiate between mission, values, and vision as follows. The *mission* of the company says something about its long-term purpose. It is a general statement of why the enterprise exists. *Values* are also long term and general in nature, and describe how the company is to be run. The emphasis is on be-

FIGURE 1.3

Mission, Vision, Values, Strategy

Mission
What is our long-term purpose?

Vision
Where do we want the business to be in 5 or 10 years?

Values
What do we stand for in our everyday behaviour?

Strategy
How do we intend to fulfil our mission and vision, while reinforcing our values?

liefs and behaviours. In contrast, *vision* focuses on the specific features of a desirable future state for the business—where you want to be in, say, five or ten years. A vision provides a reasonably specific and tangible aim, or destination, for the people in the organization to shoot for.

As indicated in Figure 1.3, all three elements are important inputs into the strategy-making process.

MISSION

A firm's mission communicates its basic identity and purpose. For example, the mission of British Airways is "To be the best and most successful company in the airline business." Some mission statements go further, indicating how the company intends to achieve its basic purpose. The mission statement of The Coca-Cola Company is reproduced in Table 1.3. Naturally enough, it focuses on the use of the brand as a key element in achieving the long-term objective of creating value for shareholders, but equally, it singles out the importance of the distribution system as a value creator.

TABLE 1.3
The Coca-Cola Company

Our Mission
We exist to create value for our share owners on a long-term basis by building a business that enhances The Coca-Cola Company's trademarks. This also is our ultimate commitment.

We exist to create value for our share owners on a long-term basis by building a business that enhances The Coca-Cola Company's trademarks. This also is our ultimate commitment.

As the world's largest beverage company, we refresh the world. We do this by developing superior soft drinks, both carbonated and non-carbonated, and profitable non-alcoholic beverage systems that create value for our Company, our bottling partners and our customers.

In creating value, we succeed or fail based on our ability to perform as stewards of several key assets:

1. Coca-Cola, the world's most powerful trademark, and other highly valuable trademarks.

2. The world's most effective and pervasive distribution system.

3. Satisfied customers, who make a good profit selling our product.

4. Our people, who are ultimately responsible for building this enterprise.

5. Our abundant resources, which must be intelligently allocated.

6. Our strong global leadership in the beverage industry in particular and in the business world in general.

There are three basic reasons for starting to work on a business mission. The first is to resolve confusion over the purpose of the business. This dilemma happens at times. Some of the most visible instances are in family-owned companies, when disagreements arise among the family shareholders over such issues as dividend income or family employment. Other examples are found in newly privatized enterprises, which have long been an arm of the state, and now have to decide on fundamental objectives, and whom they are to serve.

The second reason for developing or changing a company's mission is to revitalize it. Here the pursuit of a new mission alerts people to the need for change. In 1997 Tom Stephens took over as CEO of MacMillan Bloedel Ltd., a forest products company based in Vancouver. The company was in crisis. To stop the bleeding, Stephens moved quickly to reshape the portfolio, announcing, for example, that the paper division would be spun off to become a publicly traded company. But at an even more fundamental level, he changed the company's position *vis-à-vis* the society in which it operated. He talked, as no CEO ever had before, of MacMillan Bloedel becoming the "most respected and environmentally responsible forest products company in Canada, and an example for others globally."[2] "The public has granted us a social licence to operate," he stated, "and they have a right to expect that we will be trustworthy guardians of their renewable resources."[3] This was a radical change in MacMillan Bloedel's mission; to this point the company had routinely engaged in clear cutting of forests, and was constantly in battle with organizations such as Greenpeace. Stephens' message was clear, both inside and outside the company: expect fundamental change.

Finally, you might decide to prepare a mission statement when your business is operating reasonably well, but you think that creating one might be useful to reinforce your existing informal "sense of mission," or perhaps as a public relations exercise, to better present the business to shareholders, customers, or regulators.

The challenge in developing a business mission is to simultaneously raise people's sights, give them direction, and stay realistic. While it usually helps to formalize agreements about mission in an explicit statement, the existence of a formal mission statement may actually mean very little; the critical factor is whether a sense of mission has permeated the organization. Achieving a powerful sense of mission depends very heavily on the day-to-day decisions and actions of a business's leaders. People look to actions, not words, for guidance. If a purpose like "to be the best and most successful company in the airline business" is to have real motivating power and directional meaning, then the actions of senior management in everything from investment decisions for aircraft to the budgets for cleaning cabins had better be consistent with it.

These comments are not in any way intended to diminish the role of formal mission statements. People expect rather a lot of written mission statements, and they are frequently disappointed when they find only the broadest of statements about generic good business practice. What does it mean, after all, for a company to say that "shareholder value comes first," particularly when virtually every other company in the industry is saying the same thing? Mission statements will inevitably be of a general nature. They simply have to encompass a wide range of circumstances and a variety of audiences.

What we can expect from them, however, are three things: that they (1) settle some fundamental questions about the purpose of the business; (2) prompt and reinforce the day-to-day actions that are consistent with their meaning; and (3) provide direction in the formulation of the more specific vision and strategy of the firm.

VALUES

A corporate values statement presents the basic beliefs that govern individual and group behaviour in an organization. This may be brief and at a high level of abstraction, or much more detailed and specific. Bill Hewlett, one of the founders of Hewlett-Packard, made the following statement in the early 1940s to define what he called "the HP way": *I feel that in general terms it is the policies and actions that flow from the belief that men and women want to do a good job, a creative job, and that if they are provided the proper environment they will do so.* This statement has remained at the heart of HP's values ever since, and it has now been supplemented by a set of five more specific organizational values, shown in Table 1.4.

At first glance, you may find this a rather straight-forward list. There is certainly very little here to disagree with. Surely every company wants a high level of achievement from its people, wants to conduct its business with integrity, and so on. On the other hand, HP really lives these values, so one can find in the organization performance-based pay, team incentives, a first-class working environment, a heavy investment in training, a demand for employee flexibility in terms of work assignments, an intense focus on understanding and meeting customer needs, and so on. Since HP has achieved these things, then it is indeed different from many other companies. So, as with the mission statements, it is the actions that count. Creating a values list that looks good is not so difficult; living up to your values is a tougher task.

We add a final caveat on the issue of values. One might expect that an enduring set of values could only be beneficial to a company, but this is not necessarily the case. For many years under the leadership of Akio Morita, Sony Corporation of Japan operated with the strongly held core value that Sony is a pioneer, and does not follow others. This was very motivating, especially to the researchers and engineers in Sony's laboratories, and the company introduced

TABLE 1.4
Hewlett-Packard

Organizational Values

We have trust and respect for individuals. We approach each situation with the belief that people want to do a good job and will do so, given the proper tools and support. We attract highly capable, diverse, innovative people and recognize their efforts and contributions to the company. HP people contribute enthusiastically and share in the success that they make possible.

We focus on a high level of achievement and contribution. Our customers expect HP products and services to be of the highest quality and to provide lasting value. To achieve this, all HP people, especially managers, must be leaders who generate enthusiasm and respond with extra effort to meet customer needs. Techniques and management practices which are effective today may be outdated in the future. For us to remain at the forefront in all our activities, people should always be looking for new and better ways to do their work.

We conduct our business with uncompromising integrity. We expect HP people to be open and honest in their dealings to earn the trust and loyalty of others. People at every level are expected to adhere to the highest standards of business ethics and must understand that anything less is unacceptable. As a practical matter, ethical conduct cannot be assured by written HP policies and codes; it must be an integral part of the organization, a deeply ingrained tradition that is passed from one generation of employees to another.

We achieve our common objectives through teamwork. We recognize that it is only through effective cooperation within and among organizations that we can achieve our goals. Our commitment is to work as a worldwide team to fulfill the expectations of our customers, shareholders and others who depend upon us. The benefits and obligations of doing business are shared among all HP people.

We encourage flexibility and innovation. We create an inclusive work environment which supports the diversity of our people and stimulates innovation. We strive for overall objectives which are clearly stated and agreed upon, and allow people flexibility in working towards goals in ways that they help determine are best for the organization. HP people should personally accept responsibility and be encouraged to upgrade their skills and capabilities through ongoing training and development. This is especially important in a technical business where the rate of progress is rapid and where people are expected to adapt to change.

Source: www.hp.com.

a long list of innovative products, such as the Walkman, that were clear firsts on the market. The pioneering spirit was an important element of Sony's success.

In the last few years, however, concerned that it may lose its preeminent position in home entertainment as the computer business and the home entertainment business converge, Sony has chosen to develop a personal computer. Working with Intel and Microsoft, Sony's entry in the personal computer business is clearly not a pioneering move. Sony engineers have had to learn to work with others. Nobukuyi Idei, the new president of Sony, is starting to talk about modified values. His key words are *originality, passion, openness,* and *change.* Originality is closely tied to the previous pioneering concept, but openness, in particular, is a new idea, and what Idei is promoting is an openness to ideas from other companies, to soften Sony's often isolationist stance.

Values may need to change, as competitive circumstances and strategy change.

VISION

Visions give people something tangible to shoot for. An effective vision for a business articulates "a view of a realistic, credible, attractive future for the organization, a condition that is better in some important ways than what now exists."[4] An effective vision describes a possible dream—a dream that will hopefully marshal the energy, the confidence, and the efforts of all of the people in the organization.

Schindler Elevator of Switzerland has recently published its simply stated vision, *"leadership through service."* At first glance, this seems rather innocuous, and unlikely to be very motivating. However, a closer looks suggests otherwise. As Schindler is number two in its industry, behind Otis, achieving leadership in sales volume is a very challenging task. And "leadership" as Schindler defines it, also includes leadership in quality, safety, innovation, employee motivation, and responsiveness to customers. Furthermore, to ensure that the company's operating units around the world pay more than lip service to the vision, objectives are set and performance is measured in each of these areas. In terms of customer satisfaction, for example, every Schindler operation is to be ranked higher than the competition in its served markets, and at a minimum must achieve greater than 45 percent of respondents ranking the company a "5" (i.e., excellent) on a five-point scale. Less than three percent of responses are allowed at the "1" or "2" level. Similar objectives exist for employee motivation and market share position. If you work anywhere in the Schindler world, this vision is difficult to ignore.

In addition to spelling out the company's destination, which is "leadership" in its industry, Schindler's vision statement indicates how that destination is to be reached: through "service." Once again, this does not sound particularly exciting. However "service" is a motivating and differentiating concept for the Schindler organization for several reasons. First, Otis and Mitsubishi, both major competitors, have visions which emphasize leadership through technology, so Schindler's vision statement is differentiating it from its most important rivals. Second, Schindler has traditionally been a manufacturing and technology-driven company, and emphasizing that the company will compete on service is a new concept which will drive change in many areas of the organization. Finally, as Peter Zbinden, the president of Schindler, commented:

> When we say "service," we mean service to both internal and external customers. So this is a statement about how we will work together, as well as how we treat our customers. The difference between a good company and a great company today is the way it delivers its overall service. Our vision captures both where we are going and how we are going to compete.

The most useful business visions also contain a time dimension. A brief vision statement, like Schindler's "leadership through service" may sound similar to a mission statement, but the difference is that a vision has a timetable that helps to create a more concrete and compelling picture. There is a great deal of overlap, but also a significant difference, for example, between a statement of a mission "to be the best and most successful company in the airline business," and one that states, "by the year 2000, we will be the largest and most profitable airline in the world." In Schindler's case, the company sets very specific three-year objectives tied directly to its vision statement. These are renewed and extended annually, and provide what the company calls "measurable feedback on progress made towards achievement of the company's vision."

Visions and visionary ideas may arise from a variety of sources, ranging from the singular imagination of a strong leader to an elaborate process of employee involvement. If you tap the knowledge and aspirations of the key people of an organization, the argument goes, you can achieve creativity and commitment at the same time. Indeed, if the process is carefully managed this can be true, but there are some risks and limits in this approach that should be recognized.

One management group went through a very elaborate visioning process and were quite disillusioned by the outcome. They had just spent a lot of time and effort trying to define their company as they thought it should look five years in the future. The process even involved a technology by which they could vote secretly on specific suggestions as they came up in the discussions! Ultimately a "vision" was produced which represented the mechanical consensus of the group. Then the difficulties surfaced. Some managers thought the outcome was ridiculous because it failed to properly recognize the constraints under which the company was operating. Others found it simply irrelevant—it seemed to have little to do with the very real problems that they were facing right now. Everyone was disappointed. This was a process gone wrong. The construction of a vision, any vision, had become the object of the exercise, at the expense of a real debate about the opportunities and problems in front of the company and what should be done about them.

Vision-Check

There are two basic questions to put to an emerging vision. First, does it portray a desirable *and* feasible destination? Second, does it do so without jeopardizing management's flexibility to manoeuvre as circumstances change? The question of desirability is much easier to answer than that of feasibility. For desirability, just ask people. For feasibility and flexibility, however, you need to do some careful analysis.

Feasibility   The question of whether you can reasonably expect to get to your visionary destination can't be answered in the abstract. A vision can't stand on its own. You need to relate it to the realities of the situation that it is addressing. To do this, you need to first express the vision in the more definitive terms of a supporting strategy, and second, test that strategy to see if it makes sense.

Flexibility   Much of the power of a vision lies in the fact that it is a public commitment for the whole organization. But a vision is also a perishable commodity, in part because it has its own time frame, but more ominously because circumstances may change in unanticipated ways. Management may hesitate to change a public commitment that is no longer appropriate. And even if management does change its position, the momentum behind the now obsolete vision may persist in various parts of the organization for reasons ranging from ignorance to disagreement to wilful pursuit of self-serving activities.

A powerful vision that grasps an organization also makes it difficult to turn quickly, and this risk must be considered before an organization is fired up to pursue it. As with feasibility, this risk of an inflexible visionary commitment can only be thoroughly identified by going through the steps of putting the vision in strategic terms and checking for sustainability.

FROM MISSION, VALUES, AND VISION TO STRATEGY

Missions, values, and visions are very useful, but also very general leadership tools. Properly developed, they will inspire an organization and give it a basic sense of direction and broad guidelines for getting there. But the realities of general management—which call, among other things, for judgments about the precise viability of ideas in a competitive market, the resolution of often conflicting interests, and the achievement of change in the face of inertia and resistance—demand a more precise tool to deal with ends and means, and this is what we attempt to capture in the idea of strategy, the topic of the next chapter.

15

SUMMARY

This chapter has concentrated two aspects of the general manager's job that need attention before you become immersed in the strategy-making process: assessing performance and setting the direction for the business. We suggest that your performance assessment focus on both operating performance and organizational health. Both need to be understood before you turn to strategy. In terms of direction setting, we have concentrated on mission, values, and vision. These things do not need to be written, but they do need to be agreed, and shared within the organization. Without them, you will be creating strategy in a vacuum.

NOTES

1. For a useful approach to creating multiple performance measures see Robert S. Kaplan and David P. Norton, "The Balanced Scorecard—Measures That Drive Performance," *Harvard Business Review*, (January–February 1992).

2. *Globe and Mail,* January 1, 1998.

3. ibid.

4. Warren Bennis and Bert Nannus, *Leaders: Strategies for Taking Charge* (New York: Harper and Row, 1985), p. 89.

ADDITIONAL READINGS

Performance Assessment

KAPLAN, ROBERT S. AND DAVID P. NORTON, *Balanced Scorecard: Translating Strategy Into Action.* Boston: Harvard Business School Press, 1996.

SIMONS, ROBERT, *Levers of Control.* Boston: Harvard Business School Press, 1995.

Mission, Values, Vision

BARTLETT, CHRISTOPHER AND SUMANTRA GHOSHAL, "Changing the Role of Top Management: Beyond Strategy to Purpose," *Harvard Business Review* (November–December 1994).

CAMPBELL, ANDREW, MARION DEVINE, AND DAVID YOUNG, *A Sense of Mission.* London: Hutchinson Books Limited, 1990.

COLLINS, JERRY AND M. PORRAS, *Built to Last.* New York: HarperBusiness, 1994.

DE GEUS, ARIE, "The Living Company," *Harvard Business Review* (March–April 1997).

LANGELER, GERALD H., "The Vision Trap," *Harvard Business Review* (March–April 1992).

LEAVITT, HAROLD J., *Corporate Pathfinders.* New York: Penguin Books, 1986.

STRATEGY

Strategy is a concrete expression of how a business intends to compete and win in its marketplace. As such, strategy is the definitive tool for building, communicating, and maintaining the direction of a business. The intention of strategy is to take the basic ideas of a business, such as those reflected in mission, values, and vision, and to express them in operational terms—in terms that are directly useful for analysis and action.

In this chapter we will present a practical model for developing the concept of strategy. We suggest that a useful way for you to visualize business strategy is to think of it in terms of four related components: *goals, product market focus, value proposition,* and *core activities.* After a short elaboration of this model and a discussion of its utility we will explore these building block components in some depth, one by one and then together, first in the relatively simple context of a single business, and later in multibusiness applications.

The Essentials of the Strategy Model

Our conception of strategy is presented in Figure 2.1. Taken alone, each component in this model refers to a distinct aspect of a strategy. Your first step in trying to understand the strategy of a business, or to describe its strategic intentions, is to focus on these separate components and to address such questions as the following:

1. *Goals:* What does the business propose to achieve? What are its aims, for example, with respect to growth, profitability and risk?

2. *Product Market Focus:* What are the products and/or services that the business plans to sell, and to what specific markets?

3. *Value Proposition:* How does the business intend to attract customers? What benefits constitute its "offer" or "value proposition" in the marketplace?

4. *Core Activities:* What are the primary value-adding activities that the business intends to perform and how does it intend to perform them?

As an understanding of each of the individual components starts to emerge your second step of analysis is to bring these findings together, as reflected in the schematic presentation, and to study the overall picture for clarity and consistency. If you find a reasonably coherent picture, you have the necessary base point from which to probe the past success (or failure) of the business, or to analyze its future prospects. On the other hand, if you are saddled with ambiguity you will have to start your work from scratch and deal with questions about why such a situation exists, what its consequences have been, and what needs to be done to resolve it.

The Role of the Concept of Strategy

Strategy plays a central role in the efforts of general managers to establish, sustain, and monitor the direction of their businesses. Consider the following examples of the ways in which strategy can help you out.

A Hub for Analysis   In a retrospective sense, the concept of strategy provides a base point for organizing and discussing your understanding of what a business is all about. Most businesses are more complex and subtle than they seem on first view. The concept of strategy will help you to sort out what a business is doing and what it is doing differently than its competitors, and to communicate and discuss your views on these points. And this understanding supplies a needed basis for a further analysis of why a business has been a success (or failure) and what legacy of position and momentum is implicit in this success (or failure).

In a prospective sense, the concept of strategy provides you with a starting point for analyzing and debating choices that affect the future direction of the business. There is a "base case" choice in most situations, for example, which consists essentially of pressing forward with the current strategy. Does this

FIGURE 2.1
Business Strategy Components

"base case" make sense relative to future markets and competition? What performance can you expect and at what level of risk? As you move forward, new strategic initiatives are likely to be more complex and subtle. Virtually any decision that is hard to reverse needs to be considered in relation to the intended direction of the business. Many of these emerge spontaneously as people sense an opportunity or move to deal with a specific problem. A great advantage of the strategy framework is that it helps you to highlight the ramifications of such spontaneous initiatives and to keep your subsequent analysis and decision focused on essential matters.

A Link to Action Strategy provides a vehicle for you to translate general ideas about direction and performance, for example, into more explicit, actionable terms. *Goals* set up the targets against which progress and performance can be assessed. *Product market focus* provides critical direction to people throughout the business so that they can focus their effort on targeted markets and products and, just as importantly, avoid wasting their time on tangential opportunities. Much the same can be said for the *value proposition;* this strategy component provides a beacon for employees everywhere, illuminating specifically what the business is trying to do for its customers and, by inference, the requirements of their particular role. The choice of *core activities* highlights the key jobs that will have to be done and the capabilities that need most to be developed and reinforced. Decisions to alter any or all of the components set up the requirements for achieving change.

Strategy also provides a touchstone for continuity and continuous improvement. It puts your interpretation of mission, values, and vision into a testable framework that can be used to reinforce continuity where appropriate and to drive change where necessary. In this way strategy represents a continuity of effort that can and will be changed, usually incrementally, to adapt to changing circumstances. As such it provides general managers with an everyday tool to help keep their organizations on track and to put their effort where it really counts.

STRATEGY IN A SINGLE BUSINESS

For the time being we will focus our discussion of the four strategy components by assuming that we are dealing with a single business. This business may be an independent entity or a unit in a larger corporation, but in the latter case one for which a distinct strategy is feasible—which is usually possible if it sells a distinct set of products or services to an identifiable group of customers and it is accountable for distinct revenues, costs, and investments, directly or by reasonable allocation.

GOALS

Strategic goals are an expression, in measurable terms, of what a business intends to achieve—absolutely and relative to competition. It is helpful to distinguish between two broad categories of goals, which we call *hard goals* and *soft goals*. Some examples of specific goals within these two categories are presented in Table 2.1. In this classification, the hard goals of a business focus on the aims and performance of the business as a classic competitive entity. They identify financial and marketplace targets and time frames and are relatively easy to express in measurable terms. A business, for example, may intend to grow revenues at a rate of 10 percent, be first or second in sales in the market it serves, and earn a 15 percent return on shareholder equity by year five.

The soft goals of a business set out targets for the social conduct of the business. They focus on the intentions of the business with respect to its managers, employees, and in the community at large. Soft goals may be overlooked in strategic analyses that focus too narrowly on a faceless economic concep-

TABLE 2.1
Examples of Business Goals

Hard Goals	Soft Goals
Profitability	**Management**
• Return on sales, net assets employed, and equity	• Autonomy
• Economic value added (EVA)	• Status
• Total return to shareholders	
Market Position	**Employees**
• Rank by sales, assets, etc. in industry	• Economic security
• Leader or follower in new products, marketing practices	• Opportunities to advance
• Share of market	• Working conditions
Growth	**Community**
• Increase in sales, assets, earnings	• Control of externalities
• Growth in earnings per share	• Contributions to welfare, cultural life
Risk	**Society**
• Financial risk	• General benefits through innovation, efficiency, responsible political involvement
• Operating risk	

tion of a business. And unfortunately so, for soft goals can be compelling elements for shaping the direction of a business. It would be difficult for you to develop strategy in a family firm, for example, if you did not understand the critical roles played by soft goals with respect to such matters as family status and employment.

Soft goals are also more difficult to state in measurable terms, which may be another reason why they are often overlooked. But measurability is essential if you are to understand the importance of the goal or to use it to influence the conduct of the business. There is very little point in espousing a high standard of workplace safety, for example, unless you put measures and targets and reporting systems into place.

Goal Structures

Businesses typically pursue a variety of goals simultaneously, so it is useful to think in terms of a business goal structure. In general, a goal structure should represent in scope and balance the important aims of the business. This would be true, for example, if they reflected the "balanced scorecard" notion proposed by Kaplan and Norton[1] which requires a consistent, broadly based set of goals that reflect a firm's ambitions. When this applies, as we pointed out in Chapter 1, there is a natural and easy tie to performance measurement. More often than not, however, the construction of a coherent goal structure is a tough job that calls for some very serious decisions.

Building a Goal Structure

As goals proliferate, so too do the opportunities for conflict and confusion. It is important to develop a goal structure for a business that sets priorities and minimizes conflicts. Take the very simple and common conflict that arises between short-term and long-term results: are you after profit today, which might mean lower growth, or growth today, which might mean lower current profits? If goal conflict of this nature is allowed to persist then people will be truly confused about the real aims of the business.

As you go about developing the goal structure of a business you may have to resolve some difficult conflicts between the external forces on the business and its internal interests and capabilities. External forces are represented, for example, by competitive challenges or shareholder demands. Internal influences arise from such factors as the expectations and limitations of the firm's employees. You are now well into the process of strategy formulation. Further, as circumstances change, so, too, must the goal structure.

Consider an absolutely classic example of the need to adapt goal structures to a changing environment. For decades and through to the early 1980s, IBM had put a high priority on goals associated with employee welfare, such as continuous employment and promotion from within. This worked well for many years. But then the structure of the industry changed quite rapidly, and IBM was faced with the need to change its goal structure to give precedence to market responsiveness at the expense, if necessary, of employment stability. Faced with this choice, IBM faltered. Its failure to change its goal structure to match the new circumstances caused a destructive corporate crisis with impacts well into the 1990s.

Goals and Competitive Differentiation

Businesses may elect to use their goal structures as a way of achieving competitive differentiation and advantage. Suppose, for example, that three businesses choose goal structures that are different from their competitors in their reflection, respectively, of patience, the pursuit of market leadership, and opportunism.

The patient business, for example, may be ready to absorb minimal short-term returns for the promise of significant long-term payoffs. Its willingness to invest in market development and new technology for the long haul might represent a significant advantage relative to competitors who choose, or are compelled by their circumstance, to seek faster paybacks. Fuji Photo Film's 15-year assault on Kodak in the North American photographic market is illustrative. Up to the early 1980s Kodak appeared to have a lock on the North American market. Fuji's entry was modest, but it persevered and slowly but surely gained share from Kodak. Kodak, in response, seemed continuously to be caught in a conflict between protecting its market position or protecting its profitability, with the result that its actions were often late, inadequate, or ill-conceived. This indecision has gone on for some time and, should it continue, Kodak will have literally squandered its immense starting advantage in the market.

A business that is intent on leading its market may well try to dominate its industry by playing a forceful, if risky, hand in standard setting and demand development. The willingness of such a business to assume risks, to take stands, and to blitz rivals constitutes a significant advantage over competitors who are rather more hesitant to go to the wall—so long as the business makes the right bets! Microsoft's approach to leadership in the software industry bears some resemblance to this orientation.

Finally, an opportunistically driven business tries to get into a market while it is hot, make a quick hit and then move on as the situation cools off. Such quickness of foot might result in a significant advantage over more conventional competitors who are accustomed to due process and continuity. The advent of a multitude of Internet service providers is a case in point; many of these businesses will disappear as larger, conventional telecommunication firms move into this market and spend heavily to build share and make acquisitions, but a significant number of opportunists will do so with full pockets!

PRODUCT MARKET FOCUS

The product market focus component of strategy spells out the nature of the products and/or services that a business intends to offer and the characteristics of the markets that it intends to compete in. Think of your favourite radio station. What is its emphasis in programming (rock, rap, country, easy listening, etc.) and from this, who is the implied audience (demographics, shopping habits, etc.)? Your answer will be a pretty good indication of the station's choice of product market focus.

The usual application of the product market focus concept is in looking downstream at choices of product line scope, customer groups, geographic areas, and so on. This is where a business faces the most obvious competition and where, as a consequence, the strategically most important distinctions need to be made. However, in resource industries, equally critical competition occurs on the upstream side, where businesses must compete for access and continuity of supply for oil, timber, minerals, and like reserves. In 1996, for example, Inco was locked in a competitive bidding situation with other nickel producers for access to the potentially rich Voisey's Bay nickel deposit. It secured the rights, but at a price of $4.3 billion that has come to be seen as a strategic blunder and to haunt the company as nickel prices have fallen and operating access to the deposit have been delayed by political and environmental conflicts. The important point here for your analytic process is to concentrate your product market definition on the markets—either upstream or downstream—in which the business is facing the keenest competition.

Describing Product Market Focus

If you are dealing with a business that encompasses multiple products and markets, you will find it helpful to visualize the product market focus using a cross-reference format, or *matrix,* that arranges product entries against market segments. By entering appropriate classification data into the cells of this matrix (revenues, assets employed, profits, etc.), it is possible to build a quite precise picture of the current or intended product market emphasis of the business. The example that follows illustrates the major steps in preparing such a matrix.

Building a Product Market Matrix: An Example   Olympia Mills produces a line of tufted carpets in its Spokane facilities. The carpets are sold throughout the northwest market area. One conception of the company's product market matrix is illustrated in Table 2.2. In this matrix the product and market categories were chosen to represent aggregates that Olympia could do something about in a strategic sense—such as dropping a line, or changing segment emphasis by, say, greater sales representation.

TABLE 2.2
Olympia Mills Product Market Matrix ($000 000)

	Retail	Residential	Commercial	Total
Total Revenue	5.2	13.8	3.3	22.5
Share Regional Market	6%	23%	5%	11%
Solid-Colour Carpet Revenue	3.8	11.0	1.0	15.8
Share Solid-Colour Market	9%	31%	6%	16%
Multicolour Carpet Revenue	1.2	2.8	2.3	6.3
Share Multicolour Market	3%	12%	5%	6%
Foam-Backed Market Revenue	.4	—	—	.4
Share Foam-Backed Market	—	—	—	—

The product line distinctions in Table 2.2 were chosen on the basis of manufacturing requirements and marketing considerations. Solid-coloured carpets could be tufted from yarn that was spun in the company's spinning mill and dyed in the carpet mill. This product type was particularly favoured by the residential contract market. Multicolour carpet was produced from pre-dyed yarns and was particularly important for the commercial market. Foam-backed carpet required special equipment and was suited to the lower-priced segments of the retail market.

The market segment distinctions in the matrix were chosen to reflect differences in product requirements, buying processes, and competition. The retail segment represented sales through retailers to home owners, largely for replacement. A wide style, colour, and quality range was required together with fast, reliable delivery. The residential contract market comprised sales through builders to new-home buyers and required sharp pricing to match competition on large orders. The commercial market consisted of sales for new or replacement carpeting to commercial real estate developers and their tenants. It frequently involved custom design and specifications by job.

The data chosen for the cells are indicative rather than complete. The share-of-market figures are based on the geographic market served. Additional information on product line contribution, assets employed, total market potential, etc., might be useful for further analysis.

The classifications clearly involve a number of judgments. Why weren't the products broken down into further quality and style classifications? Why wasn't the retail market classification further developed, for example, to identify sales direct from the mill to retailers as compared to those made through distributors? You might ask a host of other reasonable questions, for which the answer is essentially that the classifications are a matter of judgment based on an understanding of the purpose at hand. What we have described at this point is a business that is heavily reliant on the solid-coloured/residential contract market. The classifications can be further refined as emerging strategic questions and choices dictate. There are no issues of right or wrong in building a product market matrix, only those of utility.

Product Market Focus and Competitive Differentiation

A business may select a particular product market focus as a way of achieving competitive differentiation and advantage. A quite typical choice, for example, is to concentrate on product market niches where competitors are relatively weak.

McCain, for example, used this approach to built its worldwide french-fried potato business. Over a period of three decades the company moved from its Canadian base to England, Australia, continental Europe and on, all the while taking advantage of weaker competitors and avoiding the strong and entrenched competitors in the U.S. marketplace. Then, in the mid 1990s, the company, which was now well armed in scale and technology, was ready to make a serious commitment to the U.S. domestic market.

VALUE PROPOSITION

A business's value proposition is a statement of the fundamental benefit or benefits that it has chosen to "offer" in the marketplace. A stockbroker, for example, may choose to focus on low transaction costs, a computer printer business on being first to market with new features, a parcel delivery business on flawless reliability. Whatever the specifics, the aim in describing the value proposition is to capture the commitment or bet, if you will, the business is making that it will attract customers.

Describing Value Propositions

The key to a useful expression of the value proposition of a business is to work with variables that are important to customers and to simplify to basic themes. Customers are interested in what a product or service does for them. They don't particularly care, for example, that a business has a goal of being the industry's low cost producer. This is only important to the customer if the low costs get translated into low relative prices or other benefits. The aim therefore should be to express value propositions in terms of fundamental customer benefits such as price, features, and execution.

It is also important to stick to simple, fundamental themes, which may be quite a task since there are a variety of ways in which a basic value proposition may be presented in a market, as illustrated in Table 2.3. A value proposition based on price, for example, might be delivered by any of a combination of dozens of direct price or indirect economic benefits. From a strategic stand-

TABLE 2.3
Subsidiary Value Proposition Variables

Price	Features	Execution
Direct	**Tangible**	**Availability**
• List price	• Quality	• Timing
• Discount structure	• Performance	• Convenience
• Rebates	• Proprietary properties	• Delivery
• Credit rates	• Pre- and post-sale service	**Reliability**
Indirect	• Options, choice	• As promised, when
• Financial assistance	• Guarantees	promised, etc.
• Capital vs. operating cost balance	**Intangible (Image)**	**Intensity**
	• Design	• Sales hustle
• Life cycle cost	• Fashions	• Service hustle
• Cost absorption (delivery, training, etc.)	• Prestige	• Friendliness
	• "Personality" and "event" associations	

point, however, the important reality is that the business's value proposition is based on price. The precise tactics for conveying these benefits are important, of course, but only after the fundamental approach has been established.

Ultimately, the scope and detail required in expressing a value proposition rests on the utility of the result. The critical question is whether the value proposition, as described, is sufficiently developed to provide a meaningful sense of direction and to support subsequent tests for effectiveness, feasibility, and sustainability. For example, you might find a proposal to compete on "customer intimacy"—a concept developed by Treacy and Wiersema in their book *The Discipline of Market Leaders*[2]—too vague to work with. The need here would be to press further and to define the particulars of relationships proposed between business and customer that lie behind the expression. On the other hand, pushing for detail, particularly in the early steps of evaluating or building a strategy, might bog you down in incidentals and restrict your flexibility. It usually makes sense to start with a very basic theme and incorporate greater detail as necessary as the analysis proceeds.

Finally, by redefining the "customer" we can apply the idea of value proposition to supply (upstream) markets. Thus, a junior oil company might define the private or governmental holders of mineral rights in a particular area as its customers and address the question of the value proposition it intends to put forward to secure those rights. Or a residential real estate business might target top rate agents as its supply side customers and address the value proposition by which it intends to secure and hold those resources.

The Value Proposition and Competitive Differentiation

The choice of a value proposition is perhaps the most obvious way in which a business attempts to differentiate itself from competition. To the extent that a proposed value proposition is important to customers, different from competitors, and hard for competitors to match, it will constitute a competitive advantage. Consider the following examples.

Discount brokerage was pioneered by Charles Schwab in the United States and the Toronto Dominion Bank's Green Line Investor Services in Canada. Their beginning value proposition was very simple—lower cost transactions than those available through traditional brokerage channels. This was a powerful proposition for many customers and it gave Schwab and Green Line a competitive advantage and an impressive start in their markets. And, over the years, they have sustained their leading positions in the face of a rash of look-alike competitors; the value proposition has become more elaborate, but the core benefit of providing the most economic channel for securities trading has remained at the centre of their success.

The value proposition of Hewlett-Packard's computer printer business focuses on being first to market with superior features, such as speed and text and graphics production quality. The March 1998 issue of *Consumer Reports,* for example, evaluated the fundamental features of ink-jet printers and rated the Hewlett-Packard DeskJet 722 as a "best buy." A clear win in differentiation and advantage for Hewlett-Packard to savour, but not for long. The company must work continuously to maintain advantages like this in a fast-changing industry.

In many industries it is relatively easy for competitors to quickly copy new product or service innovations. What major parcel service doesn't promise the equivalent of Federal Express's "world on time" slogan? What real estate company doesn't promise the best in personal attention and advice? To differentiate in such circumstances, a business may put a more subtle value proposition to work—the fact that it will actually deliver on its promise, that it will be superior in execution. What differentiates such companies is not their claim to fast service or personal attention or whatever, but the credibility of their claims, and behind this the building of businesses that can actually execute the promises better than their competitors.

CORE ACTIVITIES

In the "value chain" of activities that constitutes an industry, a business needs to make choices of which particular activities it intends to perform and how it intends to perform them. For some time now, for example, General Motors, Ford, and Chrysler have employed quite different strategies with respect to parts supply. Towards one end of a spectrum, General Motors has considered parts supply as a core activity and has internally manufactured a high percentage of its own parts, minimizing its reliance on outside suppliers. Towards the other end of the spectrum, Chrysler has deemed parts supply to be a non-core activity and has outsourced a high percentage of its parts requirements, leaving it with a heavy reliance on external suppliers. Ford has traditionally sat somewhere between these two positions.

A firm's determination of its core activities will have a fundamental impact on its market and operations control, cost structure, capabilities, and flexibility. Chrysler's decisions to rely on external parts suppliers have reflected a priority on high flexibility and low fixed costs over high control and low variable costs. General Motors has come to regret its decisions, taken years ago, to go with a highly integrated parts system because, quite to the opposite of its intentions, it has ended up with the worst of all possible worlds—high fixed costs, and because of management and labour difficulties, high variable costs, low flexibility, and inadequate control! Through the entire span of the 1990s, General Motors has been working to reduce its reliance on internal sourcing, but it has been slow going in the face of management inertia and labour opposition.

Describing Core Activities

The challenge in describing the core activities component of a business strategy is in determining the degree of scope and detail that suits the issues being considered. The scope of issues may vary from the very broad perspective of a business dealing with fundamental matters of vertical integration to the very specific process perspective of a firm considering the best way in which to weave together internal and outside activities in building a sales and service system. The focus and detail utilized in identifying and analyzing core activities should vary accordingly. In the examples below we have illustrated this principle for what we might call broad, intermediate, and process levels of generality.

In pursuing issues of vertical integration, for example, you will have to decide on what basic building blocks in the industry value chain you intend to perform and those you will access through a market. From this broad perspective, your core activities would be best described in terms of the building blocks that represent fundamental aspects of the industry such as raw material supply, primary processing, and so on. In the aluminum industry this might mean working in terms of mining, power generation, refining, semifinished product fabrication, finished product fabrication, and distribution. Alcan, for example, has for decades followed a strategy of performing all of these activities through to finished product fabrication, but here it has vacillated from period to period on whether this building block was core or not so, and in the process has gone through some confusing turns of strategy. The broad, building block approach described above is usually sufficient for industry studies and basic corporate decisions on vertical integration.

If you are trying to determine how best to proceed in pursuing a particular product market opportunity, however, the focus and detail of the core activity description will probably have to move to a functional base and deal with such categories as product and process research and development, component supply, assembly, marketing, distribution, sales and service, and so on. The aim at this intermediate level of analysis is to identify where the business has material and realistic opportunities to perform or not to perform a function and the consequences of the choices that it might make on these matters. In setting up its regional jet aircraft business, for example, Bombardier chose to focus on design, testing and systems coordination, final assembly, and marketing, and to bring in partners for manufacturing, such as Taiwan's Aerospace Industrial for mid- and rear-section fabrication and Japan's Mitsubishi Heavy Industries for wing production. These core activity choices by Bombardier represented a strategic trade-off of potential value added and control, particularly in wing manufacturing technology, for greater financial and manufacturing capacity, and possible market access.

In the broad and intermediate levels of generality the emphasis is on describing the basic activities that a business has chosen to perform and less so on how it intends to link and perform them. At the process level the focus turns to mapping activity *systems* in sufficient detail to support operations planning and coordination, systems development, and quite detailed comparisons with competitors. Here, of course, it is possible to elaborate the description into dozens and even hundreds of different, but still reasonably significant, activities. A process level comparison of the order taking, processing, and fulfilment systems for personal computers employed, for example, by Monorail, which contracts out manufacturing, Gateway 2000, which focuses on the assembly of purchased components, and IBM, which operates with relatively high integration, would reveal significant differences in their fundamental competitive strategies. As you proceed to more detailed descriptions, however, you will be faced with the question of how far to take the analysis. At some point your elaboration of the activities goes beyond major commitments that are hard to reverse and the analysis becomes more operational than strategic. This is where you stop. That is not to say that the operational issues are not important, just different, and subject to prior decisions on strategic position. For the most part, for strategic analysis and action the intermediate levels of scope and detail will usually be sufficient and should certainly be the starting point. Further detail can then be pursued as specific situations warrant.

Core Activities and Competitive Differentiation

In most industries there are many potential differences in the core activity sets that a business might choose to perform. This provides an equivalently wide range of possibilities for differentiation and competitive advantage. To illustrate, consider the choices with respect to vertical integration that are open to a business as it seeks advantages in market or supply control, cost, focus, and flexibility.

Vertical integration forward, for market control, or backward, for supply control, may provide a business with an advantage over its rivals. In the pharmaceutical industry, for example, Merck and Company, a successful research, manufacturing, and prescription drug marketing company, integrated forward to incorporate distribution as a core activity by acquiring Medco Containment Services, a mail-order pharmacy and prescription-benefits-management (PBM) company. The acquisition was a rich one, costing Merck $6.6 billion, a price which was 2.5 times Medco's sales and 45 times its earnings. It was followed in short order with similar PBM acquisitions by SmithKline Beecham and Eli Lilly. What was going on? After a review of the many and often high-minded rationales for the acquisitions, Anita McGahan arrived at a simple conclusion: "the most compelling logic for the acquisitions is that the PBMs provide the pharmaceutical companies with opportunities to increase market share as prices decrease across the industry."[3] They were attempts to secure advantage through the market control afforded by internalizing the distribution activity.

The pursuit of advantageous costs may be the critical driver behind the choice and structuring of core activities. A key element of Wal-Mart's strategy over the years, for example, has been to pursue low cost by internalizing all of the key activities in its supply and distribution value chain. This system ranges from suppliers, who are "virtually" integrated with Wal-Mart by operating policies and electronic data interchange, through the logistics functions of warehousing and transportation, to store operations and ultimately the checkout counter. As a pioneer of this approach, Wal-Mart built up a significant cost leadership over its less integrated and rigorously managed competitors and it has managed to maintain this advantage for decades!

There are limitations, of course, to the pursuit of competitive advantage by internalizing the basic building blocks of an industry. Many businesses set aside the potential benefits of vertical integration in order to focus their efforts on what they see as particularly critical activities in the industry value chain. In the athletic footwear market, for example, the big brands like Nike, Reebok, and Adidas have built formidable capabilities in design, sourcing, and marketing, but they rely on contract manufacturers for supply and independent retailers for distribution. Trade-offs of control are inevitable. Nike might *like* to control distribution, for example, and it even goes so far as to run a few megastores and a chain of factory outlets, but it simply doesn't make sense to disperse its resources in an attempt to build and maintain a major proprietary distribution operation.

Another counterbalance to the pursuit of control or low cost advantages through vertical integration is in the loss of flexibility that is incurred as a business increases its fixed commitments to activities that may be hard to exit. In the forest products industry, for example, MacMillan Bloedel for years pursued a strategy of integration from its timber operations through end products such as corrugated containers. In theory this offered competitive benefits in cost and control, but as demand and competition changed in the various activity areas over time it became an unwieldy system, marked by high fixed costs and loss-making business areas, from which it was difficult to find an escape.

Putting the Strategy Components Together

In the process of creating and testing new strategic ideas it is often useful to focus your thinking on only one or two of the four strategy components at a time. A proposal for a business to compete on price, for example, requires considerable development and analysis in its own right before it is subjected to wider scrutiny. At some point, however, you will have to pull all of the strategic components together, to see if they present an internally consistent and comprehensive picture of the direction of the business. This total view of strategy is a critical step in building an accurate understanding of a business and in evaluating its future development.

Consider, for example, the comprehensive, if simplified, version of Wal-Mart's strategy as pictured in Figure 2.2. An overview like this is intended to help you to simultaneously grasp several dimensions of a very remarkable business. You can better appreciate the power of the company in the marketplace as you observe the consistency of the strategy components from the goals of achieving low cost by pursuing its unique "Wal-Mart" way, to the product focus on basic branded

FIGURE 2.2

The Wal-Mart Business Strategy

merchandise, to the value proposition of everyday low prices and on to delivery through a highly integrated set of core activities. You have the basis in such a conception of Wal-Mart's strategy to pursue your understanding of the path that the company has followed in the past and to ask if this direction makes sense for the future. Further, you have the grounds to check out the consistency of the individual components as they stand, or as proposed for change. Suppose, for example, that it was proposed to change Wal-Mart's branded product focus and significantly increase the proportion of private or unbranded merchandise in the merchandise mix. However attractive the potentially higher margins of such a step might appear in the abstract, the first strategic test is whether this approach is consistent with the other strategy components, for example, with the need for customers to have reference points to judge the everyday low price proposition.

CORPORATE STRATEGY

The typical multibusiness corporation consists of a management hierarchy, such as that illustrated in Figure 2.3, which passes from a corporate entity to the business groups and thence to individual business units that the corporation encompasses. In this hierarchy, the corporate office establishes a corporate strategy and from this a set of strategic guidelines for the groups. The groups, in turn, develop group strategies and set up guidelines for their individual units. In general, as you move down this hierarchy from the corporate level to the unit level, the emphasis passes from broad positions to increasingly specific initiatives. Andrews, looking at the hierarchy from the bottom up, has put the distinctions very nicely:

FIGURE 2.3
A Multibusiness Strategy Hierarchy

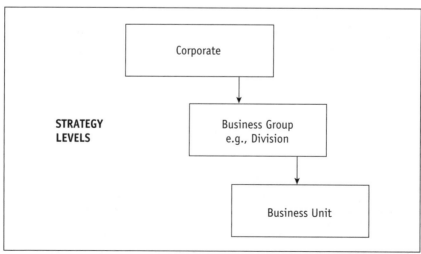

"As we ascend from a specific strategy to a corporate strategy, we pass from specific economic objectives to broader organization goals. More weight is given to such characteristics as unity, coherence, consistency, purpose, and concern for the future. The time horizon grows more distant and market-share percentages give way to a more comprehensive vision of the company's future development as an institution."[4]

The corporate level of the multibusiness organization is an intermediary—it stands between the individual businesses and the capital markets. As such, it must address one vital question—what is it that the corporate office does that results in the businesses under its umbrella being worth more than they would be standing independently, or held by another more effective corporate group? From a shareholder perspective, what is the economic justification of the multibusiness structure? Corporate strategy is an explication of the way in which the corporate entity intends to compete by providing superior shareholder value relative to these alternatives.

The critical decisions in setting the direction of a multibusiness corporation can be captured by the same four-component strategy model that we have used with individual business units. Some accommodations in the development and the expression of the individual components are necessary to handle the higher levels of aggregation, but the basic purpose and nature of the components remains the same.

Corporate-Business Unit Strategy Relationships

The relationship between corporate and business unit strategy is illustrated in Table 2.4. Corporate strategy sets a broad, common direction. It serves to spell out the corporate position on aggregate goals, on what constitutes a desirable

TABLE 2.4
Examples of Corporate-Business Unit Strategy Relationships

Strategy Component	Key Corporate Strategy Questions	Business Unit Implications
Goals	Aggregate needs and ambitions	Stretch, flexibility in business unit goals
Product Market Focus	Composition of portfolio of businesses	Business unit role and boundaries
Core Activities	Corporate vs. business level management responsibilities	Management relationship to corporate
Value Proposition	Related vs. unrelated value propositions	Priorities, boundaries for unit value proposition

business unit portfolio, on the management activities that the corporate office should perform, and on the substance of any shared value proposition.

A business unit strategy in this context is, in the first instance, a response to a corporate strategy. But the relationship is not that simple. In healthy organizations there is a good deal of give and take between the corporate and subordinate levels. Corporate offices propose guidelines based on aggregate needs and their reading of circumstances and business units propose initiatives based on the specific opportunities and problems that they see.

In the following section we will illustrate two very different corporate strategies and illustrate how these differences impact on strategy formulation at the level of the individual businesses.

Two Corporate Strategy Examples

Consider the differences reflected in the corporate strategies of ConAgra, Inc., the $24-billion agribusiness firm, and 3M, the $14-billion manufacturing company. ConAgra seeks to create value by selectively acquiring businesses and then improving their performance as independent operating companies by means of aggressive financial management. 3M's strategy is quite different. 3M attempts to create value by carefully nurturing the development and sharing of many specialized technologies and products over time among its many constituent business units. For exposition we will refer to these contrasting approaches as the independent portfolio and the interdependent portfolio corporate strategies.

The Independent Portfolio Strategy

In 1998 ConAgra was a diversified international food company with an impressive record of growth in revenues and profitability. The corporation consisted of over 60 independent operating companies, called IOCs, organized into five major operating groups. This portfolio of companies had been assembled over a period of 20 years in a process that involved virtually hundreds of acquisitions, joint ventures, and divestments. ConAgra regularly had about 80 candidate businesses on its "shopping list."

ConAgra's Corporate Strategy   ConAgra had a well-developed and explicit set of corporate *goals.* The company was publicly committed to achieving specific targets for after-tax cash earnings return on equity, per share growth in earnings and dividends, and debt levels. ConAgra's ability to meet these goals was critical to its credibility in the capital markets. Translated internally these targets thus became key inputs into the process of negotiating performance expectations with the IOCs. Business level management was expected to propose aggressive plans that were consistent with its opportunities and the corporate targets, negotiate agreement with the corporate office, and then to deliver performance as promised.

ConAgra's corporate *product market focus* was quite broad in that it encompassed businesses all along the food chain from crop protection chemicals and fertilizers on one end to processed branded food products on the other. The company also operated in over 30 countries, although the United States was its primary source of revenues and profit. Beyond the common themes of food and agribusiness, ConAgra structured its portfolio to ensure that each business could be dealt with as an independent entity, competing in its own markets, on its own merits.

ConAgra's corporate management focused on two *core activities:* (1) acquisition and divestment, and (2) the implementation of rigorous business planning, performance measurement, and resource allocation processes. The common themes of food and agribusiness were deemed sufficient for the company to be able to develop the corporate expertise to support acquisition and divestment activities and to place informed pressure on the IOCs for results. Business level management was given wide scope and independence to pursue opportunities, propose investments, and operate its units. The IOCs were not directed to pursue specific synergies, for example, in trading or otherwise cooperating with each other, for this would interfere with the concept of independence. They were certainly encouraged to work with each other, however, and they were grouped structurally to facilitate potential gains through leveraging compatible products and distribution systems.

Consistent with the preceding, ConAgra did not seek to achieve any particular coherence in the *value propositions* pursued by its businesses. Within the scope of defensible business practice, the business units were free to pursue the value propositions that they thought were most important in their particular markets.

ConAgra's corporate strategy presents a clear and consistent picture of the way in which the corporate entity intends to compete and add value. The company's performance to date suggests that it is indeed living up to its promise. It is quite plausible that the corporation adds value beyond that which the businesses would on a cumulative freestanding basis.

The Interdependent Business Corporate Strategy

In 1998, 3M was a well-known manufacturing company that encompassed literally hundreds of businesses and operated on a worldwide basis. The core of 3M was about 30 technology platforms—such as adhesives or precision coating—from which the company generated multiple products for multiple markets. For decades 3M had been a model for corporate innovation and had often appeared on *Fortune*'s "most admired companies list." In the late 90s, however, the company was under significant pressure—it had spun off businesses which accounted for almost one fifth of its revenues and was being hit hard by the turmoil in Asian markets. Beneath this there were questions of whether the 3M magic was still alive and whether it could produce superior results in the years ahead.

3M's Corporate Strategy   3M's corporate *goals* reflected its pursuit of the not always consistent requirements for excellence in innovation, resource utilization, market focus, and financial performance. The company was famous for requiring its businesses to produce 30 percent of their revenues from products that had been introduced in the past four years. Simultaneously it sought to be the market leader in most of its businesses and to leverage the strengths of the 3M brand. And, for financial discipline, 3M aimed at growth in earnings per share of over 10 percent a year on average, growth in economic profit that exceeded earnings per share growth, a conservative balance sheet, and the maintenance of a return on capital among the highest of industrial companies.

3M's corporate *product market focus* was established not so much by design as by a determination to allocate resources flexibly to attractive new technologies and market opportunities. Thus, while 3M's many businesses were organized into divisions, groups, and sectors, roughly on the basis of markets served, such as automotive or health services, the boundaries were far from fixed, definitive or, seemingly, even logical. Perhaps as a result, 3M was sometimes criticized for not having a strategy, but this complaint seems off the mark, in that 3M was not so much a manager of a coherent portfolio of businesses as of an evolving portfolio of technical opportunities. And when the opportunities waned, 3M was decisive (if patient) in acting—for example, in spinning off nearly $3 billion worth of computer diskette, and audio- and videotape business in 1994.

Insofar as *core activities* were concerned, 3M's corporate management focused on its 30-odd technology platforms and therein first, to feed and weed them (and aspiring new technologies as well) in relation to their potential for creating commercial possibilities, and second, to ensure that the possibilities were being exploited throughout the corporation. To the degree that these corporate efforts were successful, 3M's various businesses would be armed to achieve superior performance through their ability to compete on innovation, quality, and reliability. And since this was certainly a difficult *value proposition* to copy, 3M could lay claim to having created a sustainable competitive advantage.

The challenge for business level management in all of this was in dealing with a very complex corporate overlay—from multiple goals, to ambiguous boundaries and priorities, to limited autonomy. Recognizing this, the 3M corporate level also worked hard to nourish an elaborate culture (the word *system* is too mechanical) that was at once nourishing and demanding, patient and impatient, forgiving and ruthless, and that relied heavily, as might be expected, on the experience and wisdom of long-term managers. Scientists and business managers throughout the corporation were expected to be creative in their work, open to sharing and transferring their ideas, and effective in translating these ideas into commercially successful products and businesses.

Complex it may be, but 3M's corporate strategy has generated superior performance for many decades. If the company overcomes the challenges of the late 1990s it will have confirmed without doubt the power of its strategy to achieve superior results through the skilful management of a complex of interdependent businesses.

Corporate Strategy and Corporate General Management

The central challenge to corporate general management is to create a coherent corporate strategy—such as those we saw in the cases of ConAgra and 3M. Under these circumstances it can be seen how the businesses in the portfolio stand to benefit from their corporate association. Put another way, any multibusiness endeavour for which corporate management cannot articulate a coherent and persuasive strategy should be marked as suspect—the corporate association is probably not adding value and may in fact be destroying value as corporate politics and misdirection get in the way of the progress of the individual business entities.

The proof of the pudding, of course, as to whether a corporate strategy makes sense, and whether corporate management is doing a worthwhile job, is in performance. On this basis, for example, it would be reasonable to conclude that the corporate strategies and managements of ConAgra and 3M have merit. But performance in the case of multibusiness enterprises can be a tricky measure to pin down, because of the inherent complexity of the situation and the fact that the most relevant criterion—the potential performance of the businesses on a separate basis or with another parent—is inevitably a hypothetical estimate. This gives corporate general managers considerable licence, particularly in the short term, to fool themselves and their shareholders. An important counter in these circumstances of performance ambiguity is for corporate managers to be particularly careful that they define and work to a strategy, and for shareholders to insist on the same. In some situations this comes naturally as it did with 3M's recognition that the computer disk and video/audio tape businesses should be spun off. In other circumstances, unfortunately, the reality of a weak corporate strategy needs to be triggered by tangible events, such as a takeover threat, which, for example, preceded ICI's demerger into ICI and Zeneca, or by continuous shareholder pressure as has been the case with ITT.

SUMMARY

This chapter has concentrated on the task of identifying the strategy of a business in terms that are easy to communicate and open to logical tests. We have defined strategy in terms of four related components: goals, product market focus, value proposition, and core activities. Each of these components represents a distinct facet of strategy and each needs to be individually described and understood. We have suggested some general approaches to this task, all of which emphasize the ultimate utility of the interpretation for the strategic decisions at hand. Finally, we have emphasized the need to draw the components together to see how they relate and co-determine the direction of the business. We are now ready to proceed with the next steps of strategic analysis.

NOTES

1. Robert S. Kaplan and David P. Norton, "The Balanced Scorecard—Measure That Drive Performance," *Harvard Business Review*, vol. 70 (January–February 1992), pp. 71–79.

2. Michael Treacy and Fred Wiersema, *The Discipline of Market Leaders* (Reading: Addison-Wesley Publishing Company, 1995). The authors use the terms "operational excellence," "product leadership," and "customer intimacy" to describe the key "value disciplines" that a business might pursue. In plain English these terms are consistent, respectively, with price, features, and execution.

3. Anita M. McGahan, "Industry Structure and Competitive Advantage," *Harvard Business Review*, vol. 72 (November–December 1994), pp. 115–124.

4. Kenneth R. Andrews, *The Concept of Corporate Strategy*, rev. ed. (Homewood, Illinois: Richard D. Irwin, Inc., 1980), Chapter 2.

ADDITIONAL READINGS

COLLIS, DAVID J. AND CYNTHIA A. MONTGOMERY, "Creating Corporate Advantage," *Harvard Business Review*, vol. 76 (May–June 1998), pp. 71–83.

DONALDSON, GORDON AND JAY W. LORSCH, *Decision Making at the Top: The Shaping of Strategic Direction.* New York: Basic Books Inc., 1983.

GRANT, ROBERT M., *Contemporary Strategy Analysis.* Cambridge: Blackwell Publishers, 1995, Chapters 1 and 2.

PORTER, MICHAEL E., "What Is Strategy?" *Harvard Business Review*, vol. 74 (November–December 1996), pp. 61–78.

WRAPP, EDWARD H., "Good Managers Don't Make Policy Decisions," *Harvard Business Review*, vol. 62 (July–August 1984), pp. 2–11.

THE DIAMOND-E
FRAMEWORK

This chapter describes the basic steps involved in creating, re-vising, and evaluating strategies. We present a comprehensive model, which we call the *Diamond-E framework,* to help you identify and relate the broad forces that must be considered in building and testing strategies, and we suggest a sequence of steps for you to follow to put the model to work. In later chapters we will elaborate on the variables in the Diamond-E framework and on our suggestions for incorporating them into the creative and analytic process.

INTRODUCING THE DIAMOND-E FRAMEWORK

The Diamond-E model, as presented in Figure 3.1, is, in effect, a road map for strategic analysis. It identifies the key variables that need to be considered in the analysis and structures the critical relationships among them. Strategy is the critical linking variable in the model. Strategy tells you what opportunities the business is pursuing in the environment and by inference what resources, or-ganizational capabilities, and management preferences are required for effective implementation. The double-headed arrows in the diagram indicate that any of the variables can either drive strategy (in the sense, for example, that an envi-ronment change forces a strategy change, or that a new strategic initiative is launched to exploit a unique resource) or constrain strategy (as, for example, when resources are insufficient to support a contemplated strategic change).

Each variable in the Diamond-E relates directly or indirectly to each of the others. Within the business, for example, management preferences will directly influence strategic choices and organizational factors, and these in turn will influence resource development. The precise nature of the relationships will vary in different situations, but it is vitally important to appreciate the dynamic consequences of the linkages: changes in any one variable will likely affect all the other variables.

THE CRITERION OF CONSISTENCY

The logical principle underlying the Diamond-E framework is that of consistency, or alignment. The idea is that high consistency among the the component variables in the Diamond-E will lead to successful performance, while conflict or inconsistencies will lead to poor performance. It follows that a viable strategy needs to be in alignment with the opportunities and challenges of the environment on one hand, and with the internal capabilities, drives, and constraints of the business on the other hand. To persist with a course of action in the face of serious inconsistencies is to court disaster.

The Diamond-E model and the criterion of consistency may seem disarmingly simple. The rub is that a strategy must satisfy both the external and internal circumstances *simultaneously*. For example, a strategic initiative that addresses what seems to be a great new opportunity will be doomed to failure if it makes unrealistic demands on resources and organization.

Consider the situation facing Reto Braun when he took over as CEO of Moore Corporation, the world's largest provider of business forms and labels and associated services, in 1993. Over the previous decade, Moore's traditional strategic focus on paper-based systems had become less and less consistent with the emergence of electronic systems and with the challenges of new competitors

FIGURE 3.1
The Diamond-E
Framework

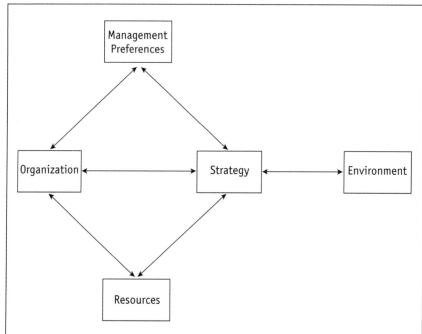

who were working with customers to develop electronic applications. Braun set out to modernize Moore, quickly. He changed Moore's strategy by putting a high priority on the new applications and their supporting technologies and he pressed forward with acquisitions and reorganization to back up these strategic moves. Unfortunately, the issue of consistency just shifted from one place to another. The new strategy was more consistent with the environment, but the demands of the strategy were too ambitious for the business to implement. Braun had taken too great a leap. Moore's performance started to deteriorate. By the time William Tyler took over from Braun in 1998, Moore was a business in crisis—it had cut its dividend for the first time in its 116-year history and had announced a plan to "shrink itself back to health" and go back to the future by revitalizing its traditional forms and labels operations.

The Moore example illustrates a further catch in the seemingly simple balances of the Diamond-E, in that the linkages must be developed and sustained over time, as circumstances change. A strategy that is in alignment for some time, even decades as was Moore's, will eventually fall into inconsistency, just as inevitably as environments change, if it, and all the other internal variables in the business, are not kept up to date.

In reality, total consistency is elusive. The variables in play are too complex and too dynamic to expect this. The principle of alignment remains the driving concern in strategic analysis, however, and it becomes a matter of management judgment to decide which inconsistencies the firm can live with, which can be resolved or mitigated within the existing strategic approach, and which are so significant and difficult to address that major strategic changes are required.

Consistency, Opportunity, and Risk

Since the principle of consistency is an ideal, virtually every strategy will be associated with some current and future inconsistencies. A critical aspect of strategic analysis, therefore, is to identify these inconsistencies and to assess the degree of risk associated with them. The risks can then be weighed against the opportunity that the initiative offers. A broad classification of the risks arising from inconsistencies is given in Figure 3.2.

Environmental risks arise from potential inconsistencies between strategy and environment. In the short run, the risk is usually one of miscalculating timing, or potential, or competitive reaction: you think that a strategic initiative will work but there is a chance that you may be misreading the situation. Is Canon's heavy investment in digital photography a sound one, for example, in light of the uncertainties about the speed of development of this market? In the long run, the risk is usually one of missing or underestimating environment changes: you think you are okay, but your perceptions are biased by past success and present ambiguity.

	TIME HORIZON	
	SHORT-TERM	LONG-TERM
ENVIRONMENTAL RISKS	Errors in reading the environment cause strategic failure	Environmental changes make the strategy obsolete
CAPABILITY RISKS	Strategic demands exceed the capacity to execute	Internal capabilities develop inconsistently with strategy

FIGURE 3.2
Strategic Risks

Operating risks arise from inconsistencies between strategy and the capabilities and drives within the firm. In the short run, a new strategy may simply demand too much. We saw that in the earlier Moore Corporation example. Or, in the long run, capabilities may not develop adequately to support a consistent but continuously more demanding strategy. A recent management change at McDonald's, for example, in which Jack Greenberg took over as CEO from 11-year veteran Mike Quinlan, was cheered by shareholders who felt that the company had become caught in a rut. The issue wasn't so much in its long-standing strategy of superior quality, service, and cleanliness, as it was in its inability to maintain its early superiority in the face of constantly improving competitors. McDonald's had stuck with its original operating formula far too long and its attempts to stay ahead were being hobbled by both inadequate and mistaken efforts to develop new restaurant delivery systems and procedures.

Bear in mind that risk is unavoidable—don't trap yourself in a fruitless quest for a risk-free strategy. Be conscious of risks, certainly, but be sure to weigh them against needs and opportunities. Strategies that intelligently stretch what is possible in the market and what is possible to implement are those most likely to provide high returns and competitive advantage.[1]

Strategy, Strategic Proposals, and Strategic Analysis

In Chapter 2 we described business strategy in terms of four related components—goals, product market focus, value proposition, and core activities. It is important for you to remember, as you describe and evaluate strategy in these terms, that you are usually dealing with the result of an evolutionary process—the cumulative outcome of a series of small steps taken one at a time over an extended period of time. It would actually be quite unusual for a strategy, as you identify it, to be the end point of some grand plan. Rather, it is more likely to be the product of a series of important but limited strategic decisions—each made on the basis of what made sense at the time. Wal-Mart's strategy, as we described it in Chapter 2, for example, was not the end result of a master plan that Sam Walton had in his mind when he started into the business, but rather of a series of smart moves that he made over the years to exploit insights and opportunities as they occurred.

What this means for strategic analysis is that as you move from diagnosis to the consideration of new ideas you will be working for the most part with one or more *strategic proposals.* Strategic proposals are discrete ideas or action plans that will have significant implications for one or more of the components of strategy and thus for the strategy of the business as a whole. An acquisition proposal, for example, may have its most significant strategic impact on a firm's product market focus. A decision on the desirability of the acquisition proposal must therefore consider whether it makes sense in terms of (1) the shift in product market focus; (2) the secondary implications of the acquisition for the other elements of strategy; and finally (3) consistency with the other variables in the Diamond-E framework. This is a big job, but at least we aren't trying to reinvent the whole strategy. Fortunately, we don't have to start from scratch to create a totally new strategy very often, although in cases of major environmental changes and company crises this is pretty much the case.

Some strategic proposals, like those that involve new product launches or acquisitions, are easily identified. Others are less obvious and may even be disguised, either deliberately or inadvertently. A division manager may, for example, push for the selection of a larger plant site, leaving submerged the questions of whether the corporation should expand, or even be in the business. Similarly, management may appraise a new compensation scheme on the basis of its equity, technical, and tax merits, but not fully explore its potential impact on the goals of the organization. The implication, again, is that you must take a broad approach to strategic analysis, remaining sensitive to the strategic implications of what may seem to be everyday decisions.

USING THE DIAMOND-E FRAMEWORK

In the description of the process of strategic analysis that follows we refer to the use of the *Diamond-E drill.* This is shorthand for a systematic review of each of the key linkages in the Diamond-E framework—strategy with environment, resources, management preferences, and organization. The objectives of the drill, depending on circumstances, are to help (1) assess the appropriateness of the firm's current strategy, (2) generate new ideas and strategic proposals, and (3) evaluate specific strategic proposals.

The Strategy-Environment Linkage

In a typical application of the drill, the first task is to deal with the strategy-environment linkage. This requires a careful analysis of the forces at work in the environment and the translation of these observations into their implications for the business in terms of specific strategic opportunities and challenges. With these opportunities and challenges in hand you can proceed to check the existing strategy of the business for consistency, to evaluate a proposal that has been put forward for analysis, or to work at generating new strategic proposals. A final step in working through the strategy-environment linkage is to put together a performance forecast for the proposal(s) under study based on the assumption (to be tested later in the drill) that it could be successfully implemented. The analysis of the strategy-environment linkage will be expanded on in Chapter 4.

The Strategy-Resources Linkage

The first step in checking the strategy-resources linkage is to identify the resource requirements for the current strategy or new strategic proposal. This is followed by a comparison of the required resources with those available, or readily available, to the business and with this the identification of resource gaps. A judgment follows on the probabilities of being able to close the resource gaps, the consequences of failing to do so, and ultimately the wisdom of proceeding with the strategy under study. In the meantime a great deal has been learned about the resources of the business and this can be woven into the process through the creation of new proposals.

This last point, the idea of coming up with new strategic proposals while in the middle of a process aimed at examining established ones, is a critical aspect of the Diamond-E drill. It emphasizes that we are not proposing a linear, closed system of logic but an open system of analysis that should recycle to incorporate learning and insights as it proceeds. In this sense, the "drill" involves much more trial and error and iterative logic than may first be assumed.

The analysis of the strategy-resources linkage is expanded in Chapter 5.

The Strategy-Management Preferences Linkage

Most models for strategic planning and analysis focus on the alignment of strategy, environment, resources, and organization. These models are fine as far as they go, but we believe that they are seriously flawed by not including the strategic preferences of the key managers in the business. Managers, after all, are the authors and implementers of strategy. Their preferences constitute strategic drives and constraints just as surely as do resources and organizational capabilities. The beliefs of Ingvar Kamprad, for example, that well-designed, well-built furniture should be available to the common family at affordable prices were of central importance in the development of IKEA's business strategy. Our position, in general, is that you can't expect to do an effective job of understanding, creating, and analyzing strategies if you leave preferences out of the picture.

The analysis of the strategy-management preferences linkage starts with the identification of the preferences that would be consistent with the successful implementation of the strategy. These are then compared with the preferences of the business managers who are critical to the implementation process. If these required and observed preferences are consistent, the analysis can move on. But there are two kinds of problems that might arise. First, you may find that the preferences of the various managers are quite similar, but at odds with the strategic proposal. The proposal may call for a significantly more aggressive attitude towards innovation and risk, for example, than is currently prevalent in the management ranks. Such a situation will call for a judgment on whether the preferences can reasonably be modified by organizational action, or whether this is just asking for too much. If the latter is the case, you may have to abandon the proposal. This would be a painful move, because any proposal that has come this far has passed the consistency checks with environment and resources.

Second, you may find that differences in individual strategic preferences is causing conflict among the managers as well as with the strategy. This is actually quite common, since managers in different roles such as marketing, manufacturing, research and development, and so on will quite naturally reflect different orientations to strategic content, timing, and risk. Recall that one of the prime functions of strategy is to get these different managers working from the same script. As you begin to understand the nature of these conflicts you can determine the best steps to bring the preferences into alignment and the time and risk factors involved in doing so.

The analysis of the strategy-management preferences linkage is expanded in Chapter 6.

The Strategy-Organization Linkage

The assessment of the strategy-organization linkage is usually the last step in the Diamond-E drill. If a proposed strategy has made it this far through the analysis you are usually reasonably happy with it, and want to determine whether the organization will implement it effectively. Thus, if you find problems in the strategy-organization linkage, your first response will be to try to change the organization to develop new capabilities. Only if this does not appear feasible should you consider changing the strategy.

You should start the strategy-organization analysis by identifying the organizational capabilities required to implement the strategy, as deduced directly by the strategy and indirectly from the gaps identified in the resource and preference analysis. The next step is to check for consistency between the required capabilities and those evident in the organization. In the happy event that these are consistent you can move on to forecast performance, make choices, and work on implementation. If there are gaps, however, you will need to determine the nature and feasibility of the the changes to develop the missing capabilities. As we will explain in Chapter 7, there are four critical variables that have a major impact on your organization's capabilities. These are leadership, structure, management processes, and culture. What changes will be required in these variables, and how difficult will it be to make the changes?

Having completed an assessment of the consistency of the strategy-organization linkage, and at least one tour around the Diamond-E, it is time to return to the conditional performance forecast coming out of the earlier strategy-environment analysis. Does the forecast stand up in the light of implementation issues? If so, the strategy and its promise can be carried forward to further comparisons and decision. If not, either the performance forecast will have to be revised to reflect the implementation issues, or the strategy itself will have to be modified and the analysis recycled.

THE PROCESS OF STRATEGIC ANALYSIS

The Diamond-E drill is the focal point of a more comprehensive process of strategic analysis as described in Figure 3.3. This is a full strategic review that works from an assessment of the current performance and strategy of the business through the creation and assessment of strategic options to decision and implementation. Such full and formal analyses are appropriate (1) on a periodic basis, such as once a year, as determined by senior management; (2) in light of current or anticipated poor performance; (3) when the business confronts a suddenly perceived opportunity or threat; or (4) to fully assess a spontaneous proposal originating within the organization.

Formal strategic reviews are very important, but there is an equivalently significant contribution to be gained from employing this same process informally on an ongoing basis. If this analytic process also becomes an informal and continuous part of the way managers think about the future of their business, there will be big dividends in the timeliness of recognizing new possibilities and in the flexibility to address them. There is no need here for numbers and surveys and presentations; rather, you try on an ongoing basis to put everyday events and experience together in a format that pushes you to think about long-term implications. Then, as circumstances unfold, you are ready for timely action or perhaps to initiate a more formal review. In this sense the process of strategic analysis, or strategic thinking if you will, becomes an integral part of the everyday agenda of management.

Activities

Step 1: Base Case Analysis Assess the strategic position of the business and the urgency for action.	1. Assess past performance. 2. Identify and evaluate current strategy using the Diamond-E drill. 3. Forecast future performance under current strategy. 4. Decide on the need, nature, and urgency of change
Step 2: Strategy Formulation and Testing Develop and evaluate proposals to address business opportunities and challenges.	1. Work from the environment and capabilities to generate new proposals. 2. Use the Diamond-E drill to shape and short-list proposals. 3. Prepare performance forecasts for short-listed proposals.
Step 3: Decision and Implementation Commit, implement, and review.	1. Decide on proposal(s) to implement. 2. Move to build commitment and develop required capabilities. 3. Implement.

FIGURE 3.3
The Process of Strategic Analysis

Whatever the initiating conditions, and at whatever point you enter the strategic review process, there are three steps or stages of work that need to be completed. In logical sequence, which you should understand may not reflect your entry point, these are (1) base case analysis, (2) strategy formulation and testing, and (3) decision and implementation. As illustrated in Figure 3.3, the Diamond-E drill is central to Steps 1 and 2 of this process. The following sections describe each of these steps.

Step 1: Base Case Analysis

The objective of this step of analysis is to establish what will happen if you simply continue to employ the current strategy, or modest variations of it, and from this the urgency for strategic action.

Assess Performance   A careful analysis of the performance of your business is a fundamental first step in base case analysis. Unless you are on the brink of a dramatic change in the environment, performance trends that are on target suggest that you have the strategy about right. Performance difficulties, on the other hand, means that your business strategy doesn't suit competitive conditions, or that your capabilities are inadequate, or both. Diagnosis will always require detective work, and a sensitive analysis of performance factors will provide essential clues to the location and the extent of strategic problems.

First, test the performance of your business against internal goals and external pressures using the measures of operating performance and organizational health that we suggested in Chapter 1. Pay particular attention to your most important strategic goals. If the generation of new products is a critical goal, how are you doing? If you need to gain market share at the expense of a certain competitor in a particular segment, ensure that you have the data you need to monitor progress. Bear in mind that these measures of performance relative to your own goals are important, but not conclusive. You will still have to evaluate, as part of your subsequent Diamond-E analysis, whether the goals, as set, are appropriate and realistic.

Second, you need to measure the firm's performance against external reference standards and benchmarks. How well is the business doing relative to the current expectations of shareholders, bankers, customers, labour markets, suppliers, government agencies, and so on? These judgments will identify the areas in which the firm is well positioned as well as those in which it is vulnerable.

The results of the performance assessment will help to set the agenda for the rest of your analysis. If the business is having difficulties, your approach should be one of diagnosing the problems and developing remedies. If the business is performing well, your approach should be to check vulnerabilities and build strategies to take advantage of new opportunities. The steps of subsequent analysis will be the same as those illustrated in Figure 3.3, but the focus will be on different issues.

Identify the Strategy   To move forward from the performance assessment you need a clear understanding of your current business strategy. This is the platform for looking outward at the environment on one hand, and inward to the company on the other hand, and for deciding what forces and circumstances should be given priority attention. Sometimes your strategy will be well formed and consistent, sometimes not. But recall that your business will always have a strategy, albeit in some circumstances implicit, incomplete, or confused. Your job here is to identify the priorities that are driving the business, whatever they are.

Evaluate the Strategy   Using your business's current strategy as a point of departure, assess the consistency of the relationships in the Diamond-E framework. What you are aiming for in this application of the Diamond-E drill is a forecast of the future performance of the business, assuming that it continues to employ the current strategy. This forecast, in effect, summarizes the impact of the consistent and inconsistent relationships that you have identified in the drill.

Decide on the Nature and Urgency of Required Changes   The base case Diamond-E drill and performance forecast will provide you with the grounds for judgments about the prospects of continuing with your present strategy. If the forecast looks good, how long can you expect it to continue? How can you make it even better? In some situations you will decide that minor changes in strategy, or in the elements of the Diamond-E supporting strategy, are all that is required, and that their urgency is low. In other cases the forecast will look pretty ugly and you will have to move very quickly to implement some radical changes in strategy and operations. And sometimes the outlook will be mostly okay but one that can be improved with relatively modest strategic action.

Step 2: Strategy Formulation and Testing

As you move to create new strategic proposals, you can rely heavily on your earlier work to dictate the issues that take priority, the time frame that you have to work in, and the rough scale of action that makes sense.

Generate Strategic Proposals   Unless you have begun the process of strategic analysis with some concrete strategic proposals in mind, you are likely to find that your primary source of new ideas is the analysis that you have just completed. As you evaluated your current performance and strategy and worked through the Diamond-E drill, you were undoubtedly struck by some new insights. Now is the time to review these, to develop a list of new opportunities and problems, and to assemble proposals that address the most attractive possibilities or the most urgent challenges. Fresh ideas may also arise spontaneously, of course, and these should be added to the inventory. In general, the more thorough the preparatory work, the better the set of options you will have to consider, and the easier it will be to create new strategic proposals.

Evaluate Strategic Proposals   The most promising strategic proposals should be assessed by means of the Diamond-E drill. This workload is not quite as high this time because you can rely on much of the analysis that you have already done in evaluating the current strategy. To make sure that the door stays open for other proposals and for new ideas, your first applications of the drill should be fast and provisional. There is no need at this point for you to make detailed, formal performance forecasts. Work with consistency and inconsistency and be pretty quick to disqualify proposals encumbered by inconsistencies. The aim at the outset is to sort the proposals quickly and to assemble a short list of the promising possibilities. Then you will need to apply the full rigour of the drill, culminating with performance forecasts.

The performance forecasts for the most attractive strategic proposals will need to be carefully reviewed. You will have to make crucial judgments about whether the performance estimates will actually be met. Are the forecasts credible? Do they reflect an acceptable balance of risk and opportunity? All things considered, which of the proposals looks the best? And finally, do you have an answer yet? Or do you have to recycle in search of a strategy that is more promising and convincing than those uncovered to this point?

Step 3: Decision and Implementation

At this stage, you may be in the happy position of having a number of new strategic proposals to choose from, all of which you find attractive. More often, managers find that they are torn between adopting one of several imperfect proposals. Whatever the situation, the time has come to make a choice. Doing the analysis that we have suggested is important, but it should not be converted into an excuse for endless delay, with calls for more and more information, more and more analysis, and so on.

When your choice is made, it is time to plan for implementation. If your choice represents a significant change to your firm, you will want to look at Chapters 9 and 10 of this book, which deal with the implementation of strategic change.

SUMMARY

This chapter has presented a general framework for strategic analysis. The Diamond-E framework identifies the basic building blocks and relationships to consider in dealing with strategy problems. The Diamond-E drill provides a systematic way to evaluate strategies in light of the critical linkages defined in the model. The drill serves as a crucial phase of a broader process of strategic analysis which encompasses a sequence of steps leading from base case analysis to strategic choice.

The emphasis in the chapter has been on basic tools and logic. Subsequent chapters will go into the substance and detail required to apply the framework and process to specific strategic problems.

NOTES

1. For a further discussion of the idea of stretch, see Gary Hamel and C. K. Prahalad, "Strategy as Stretch and Leverage," *Harvard Business Review,* vol. 71 (March–April 1993), pp. 75–84.

ENVIRONMENT ANALYSIS: THE STRATEGY-ENVIRONMENT LINKAGE

In market economies businesses must compete for survival and prosperity. They succeed if their strategies address customer needs and create competitive advantages. They fail if their strategies are inconsistent with market forces. The catch, of course, is that you have to evaluate strategy in terms of the future, not the past, and these cut-and-dried realities are much easier to see in retrospect than they are in prospect.

Your job in the crucial early phases of building and evaluating a strategic proposal is to look ahead and to evaluate the fit of your strategy with a changing environment and to forecast its performance if adopted. The primary obstacle that you will face is the sheer complexity of the forces at work and their interaction and change over time. To cut through this complexity we have set out a series of procedural steps (see Figure 4.1) that will help you to focus your analysis on the critical environmental forces and to make more robust predictions about the success of the strategy under study. They tie directly into the broader processes of the Diamond-E drill and strategic analysis that we described in Chapter 3. However, as we have noted before, procedural steps are not intended to lock you into a rigid approach; they are created for clarity of exposition and to represent a general progression of analysis. Your actual analysis will undoubtedly be much more spontaneous and iterative.

Our discussion of the strategy-environment linkage will follow the proposed analytic steps. The first task is one of preparation, of isolating the questions and the forces that are of greatest importance and of doing the background work on this subset of variables to ensure that you understand their implications. The analysis then moves to a second phase of increasingly rigorous tests of the strategy and to forecasts of its performance if adopted. The final step is one of deciding whether there is justification to carry forward the proposal, as now understood, to further phases of the Diamond-E drill.

STEP 1: FOCUS THE ENVIRONMENT ANALYSIS

The initial challenge in environment analysis is to find and to focus on the major forces that will affect the success of your strategic proposal. This begins by establishing the rough boundaries of the targeted environment (e.g., the industry or market segments); these boundaries represent what we call the *relevant environment* for the strategic proposal. Then, within this limited environment, you will need to establish a time horizon for analysis and to isolate the specific forces of demand, supply, competition, and government policy which have the greatest impact on the strategy under consideration.

Focus is critical to understanding the prospects of a strategy. Without focus it is all too easy to get lost in reams of data and long lists of possibilities, and then to become frustrated because your observations turn out to be of such little use. Naturally, there is a risk that the pursuit of focus can go too far, to the point

FIGURE 4.1
**Environment
Analysis**

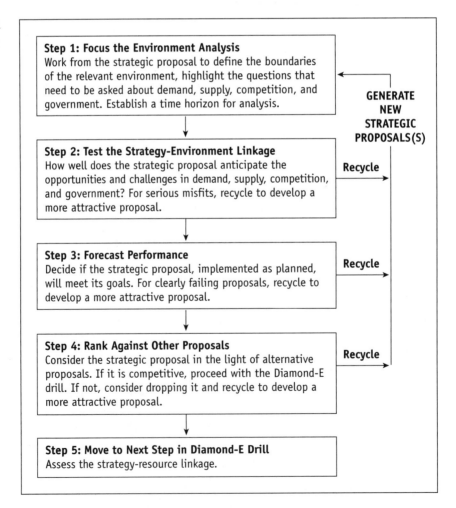

where you might miss important external facts and forces. But we believe that this is an acceptable risk, provided you are sensitive to it and employ the safeguards that we suggest for avoiding too limited an analysis.

There are three tools that you will find particularly useful in achieving a focused and properly timed environment analysis—your assessment of the performance of the business, the strategic proposal itself, and the profit model underlying the business and the specific proposal. These tools overlap in their application, in the sense that performance assessment links to strategic goals and the profit model links to core activities, but each can make a distinct contribution to the process of focusing your analysis. We will discuss them in turn below.

Performance Assessment As a Focusing Tool

As we have discussed earlier, the ongoing performance of a business sets a general context for the process of strategic analysis. As a focusing tool, your performance assessment can help you to set an appropriate time horizon for environment analysis and to indicate the range and the detail of study that suits the situation at hand. Consider, for example, the differences in focus implied for a base case analysis of the strategy of a healthy business versus the strategy of one in crisis.

The first task in the base case analysis (see Chapter 3 for a description of base case analysis) of a healthy business is one of projecting how long you expect the good times to last. A strong performance record suggests a good fit of strategy and environment. The forecasts of future performance will likely have to stretch well into the future and uncover and examine very fundamental trends. If you were involved in a base case study of Coca-Cola's strategy, for example, an appreciation of the company's outstanding record would prompt you to look well down the road for potential opportunities in market growth rates and geographic expansion, and for potential challenges from cola market saturation and the emerging competition of other beverages. Such an analysis would tie naturally into an equivalently long-term exploration of new strategic ideas, such as the prospect for Coke to enter the bottled water business. Again, the healthy circumstances of Coke would give you confidence that such an idea may well have merit and helps to justify the formidable creative and evaluative work that would be required to pursue it.

A business in crisis, on the other hand, is on a very short fuse. The base case questions go to the feasibility of a rescue effort. How much time do you have? What are the most significant problems that you have to resolve right away? Your environment analysis will have to be as immediate, tangible, and detailed as possible. In the rescue operation at the business forms producer Moore Corporation that we mentioned earlier, a fast analysis was required of the prospects of streamlining the business to focus on its core North American operations. Could the European operations, for example, be sold quickly and at a reasonable price? Was there sufficient potential in the North American market, for example, to support a struggling operation in the short run and give it a chance for revitalization? The time horizons were short and the priority for analysis was on isolating the most immediate and critical environmental forces.

The Strategic Proposal As a Focusing Tool

By its very nature, the strategic proposal that you are considering helps to identify the relevant business environment and the specific conditions on which the analysis should focus. Each of the strategy components we described in Chapter 2 has a role to play in this process:

1. Strategic goals establish the performance priorities and expectations that need to be evaluated in your environment analysis. The implications of high revenue growth targets, for example, are that you would have to ask pointed questions about the growth potential in the served market and the possibilities of increasing market share. Or, a commitment to high short-term profits would direct your attention to equivalently short-term market conditions and possibilities.

2. Product market focus sets up a bounded environment for the analysis of demand, competition, and so on. A proposal to enter a new geographic territory, for example, gives you a specific target area for pursuing questions of demand and competition.

3. A proposal's value proposition defines a very tangible benchmark for testing customer appeal and competitive differentiation. If your business chooses to emphasize price, for example, you would have to estimate the price sensitivity in the market and the capability and willingness of competitors to match or better your pricing initiatives.

4. The nature and structure of a proposal's core activities provide a basis for identifying the cost, control, and flexibility trade-offs that would be sensitive to external trends and developments. If your proposal is based on a fully integrated activity system, for example, you will have to carefully examine the potential for demand surges or setbacks since these will have a major impact on the economics of the system.

The short case study of Jantzen Technologies that follows illustrates further the role of the strategic proposal in focusing the strategy-environment analysis. Please follow this example carefully, because we will be returning to it throughout this chapter and in later parts of the book.

Jantzen Technologies: A Case Study

Jantzen Technologies is a major supplier of an important component system to personal computer manufacturers. The company was started in the mid 1980s by Harry Jantzen, an electronics engineer. Jantzen had worked for several years for a large computer company, but had become disenchanted by large company procedures and decided to strike out on his own. He had always thought there were opportunities for small companies to do a better job by out-servicing their larger rivals, and from the beginning he focused his new business on building very close technical relationships with customers and following up by continually developing new product features. The company had grown rapidly and now had production facilities in the United States, Taiwan, and Ireland to serve customers based in these areas.

By staying at the forefront of product development in a market with fast-changing requirements, and by meeting the sometimes idiosyncratic demands of its customers, Jantzen had historically enjoyed reasonable flexibility in pricing and very good profit margins. In recent months, however, negotiations with customers had become increasingly difficult. Price was becoming a much bigger factor, to the point where a major order had just been lost to an emerging competitor. There were clearly some significant changes taking place in Jantzen's business environment.

The strategic goals for Jantzen Technologies were very much a reflection of Harry Jantzen, although ownership was now substantially dispersed to the public market and employees. Growth and comfortable profit margins were paramount, not just as a matter of financial return, but to keep up the level of excitement in the company and provide the funds for continuing product development. Harry Jantzen was well known for his commitment to innovative design and for making sure that the company's development engineering staff was well taken care of. The emerging question was whether these goals were sustainable into the future.

Jantzen Technologies had taken a very deliberate approach to its product market opportunities. It had focused on a single component system, although it had always been willing to modify it or add custom features as requested by customers. On the customer side Jantzen had always concentrated on direct sales to what Harry Jantzen called the "customers who mattered," a list of a dozen or so businesses around the world which varied somewhat with the ebb and flow of the computer business. Almost as an afterthought, Jantzen sold a fairly standardized line through a major components supply house.

Jantzen's position as the leading global supplier in its field relied on innovation in product features and a willingness to work closely with individual customers and build systems customized to their particular technical specifications. Maintaining this position was a never-ending race to convert a changing basic technology into commercial systems, then to move on to the next generation of systems to stay abreast of the technology and ahead of competitors. The relationships that Jantzen's sales engineers and design teams had built with customer design teams had proved to be a major asset.

Jantzen had chosen to build a comprehensive and integrated system of core activities ranging from design through manufacturing to direct sale. This system had served to maintain close relationships with customers, proprietary control on innovations for as long as possible, and internal control over critical outputs such as quality and delivery. Plant operations in general were set up for flexibility to accommodate a high variety of custom requirements.

Jantzen's Strategy As a Focusing Tool   A base case analysis of Jantzen's prospects would rely heavily on the company's past and current strategy to provide direction on the environmental questions and conditions to explore. Here is a sampling:

1. Jantzen's growth and profit *goals* are ambitious. Is there enough growth potential and competitive room in the market to support these goals even in the short term?

2. Jantzen's *product market focus* is very narrow. With such a high reliance on a single component system and relatively few customers, it is essential to understand them thoroughly, not just in terms of their technical needs but also in terms of the economic pressures they are coming under in their marketplace. This understanding will help to build a better basis for dealing with the new negotiating pressures, and a convincing forecast based on individual customer potential and buying requirements.

3. Jantzen's *value proposition* is based on superior technical features and individual customization. This suggests two critical areas for analysis. First, will the basic technology continue to generate opportunities for product innovation? And if this window is closing, what are the competitive consequences for Jantzen? Second, will the trend towards price sensitivity continue and will this introduce new influencers and new agendas into the purchasing process?

4. Jantzen's *core activities* are highly integrated. Will this system remain cost-effective in the light of possible changes in customer purchasing criteria, and the potential development of greater competence among competitors and sub-component suppliers?

The Profit Model As a Focusing Tool

There is a profit model underlying every strategy that consists of the structure of revenues, costs, profits, and investment associated with it. You can develop the profit model for a current strategy from the actual performance records of the business. For new proposals you can develop a profit model out of the substance of the proposal, and particularly from the structure of goals and core activities. In both cases it is important to distinguish between variable costs (which vary with volume) and fixed costs (which do not vary with volume). The utility of this effort is illustrated in the following examples.

High Fixed Cost Structures   If you find that a high proportion of the costs at expected operating volumes are fixed, some special care should be given to assessing the prospects for price stability in the market. Consider the situation that prevails in the airline industry. Once an airline has set its schedule for a season its costs are largely fixed and the battle is on to maximize total contribution [volume × unit (price − variable cost)]. Since variable costs are quite low in airline operation there is a strong temptation in this structure to cut price to capture additional volume. Unfortunately, this structure leads to fierce price wars and serious profitability problems for the industry as a whole.

High Variable Cost Structures   If a high proportion of the costs at expected operating volumes are variable, however, you should take care to assess the accuracy of the assumptions about the significant input costs. Consider the problems that a large agrochemicals company has with one of its ammonia plants. The plant has a high variable cost structure and a large part of these costs are for the natural gas used in the conversion process. So much so, in fact, that the profitability of the plant hinges directly on access to natural gas at prices that are competitive with other regional producers. Some miscalculations at the time of proposing the plant about continuing political support for advantageous gas supply, however, have left this company with a major investment that simply can't make money.

High Break-Even Points   If the break-even point of your proposal is high relative to the size of the target market, you need to make a very careful assessment of your ability to achieve the required share position. But also weigh the possibility that if you do achieve the high share position, you may have established a significant barrier to new competition.

High Up-Front Investment   The timing of the investment commitments anticipated in a strategic proposal relative to the development, introduction, and market acceptance of a product will create different levels of risk. In the pharmaceutical industry, for example, much of the investment behind a new product is committed before a single dollar of revenue is received. Proposals with high up-front investment require a *very* careful assessment of market potential. In addition, the inescapable risk of such proposals suggests the need for ample supplies of risk capital. This is an argument that pharmaceutical companies use in support of patent protection—that the high returns on successful products provides the needed capital funding for the development of new products.

In the plastics products industry, on the other hand, all that may be necessary to support a proposal to introduce a new product line may be a relatively modest investment in the design and fabrication of new moulds. Often manufacturing capacity can be be built as and if the product succeeds in the market. Operating in this type of environment should certainly not be taken as an opportunity for sloppy market assessment, but there is less pressure for accuracy. The relative ease of entry, on the other hand, suggests that you must look closely at potential competitive developments.

Inflexible Investment Structures   In some cases, you will find that the nature of the investment required by a strategic proposal is such that there will be little salvage value if things don't work out. The impact of such investments on the availability and cost of capital needs to be carefully considered. A small winery that intended to age all of its products, for example, had to revise its proposal because its bankers were not prepared to finance the inventory. Similarly, a group with a uniquely designed restaurant had difficulty raising money from lenders who were concerned about the fact that the building had no alternative uses if the restaurant idea crashed. In circumstances such as these you should carefully explore the probabilities of external forces that would lead to such "worst case" scenarios.

The Profit Model As a Focusing Tool: The Jantzen Example   The Jantzen activity system, as we noted earlier, was highly integrated from design through manufacture to direct sale, and the manufacturing process itself relied on a heavy investment in specialized, computer-controlled tools to produce subcomponents. The result was a fixed cost structure that could become a serious problem if the environment became more hostile. This means that some very careful analysis must be done on the stability of market prices. What effect will maturing demand and competitive pressure have on prices? Jantzen may well have to modify its strategy to accommodate these emerging realities.

Defining the Right Time Horizon

So far, we have concentrated on picking the right questions to ask in an environment analysis. A parallel job is that of setting a time horizon for the pursuit of these questions. You will clearly have to project into the future, but how far? Earlier we mentioned the role of your performance assessment in establishing time horizons. There are three additional factors that will help: (1) the pace of change in competitive and other industry forces; (2) the flexibility of the strategic commitment under consideration; and (3) the time required to implement the new strategy.

Pace of External Change   The life cycles for products and technologies seem to have become shorter and shorter, compressing the time horizons that are relevant for environment analysis. The shorter and shorter gaps between the introduction of new versions and speed levels of Intel's Pentium microprocessor chips are a telling example of this phenomenon. Each generation of chip development changes the environment for computer builders, competitive microprocessor suppliers, and other industry participants and each generation imposes new and ever-shorter time horizons on strategic proposals in the industry.

But the pace of change varies widely from one situation to another, so gauging the speed with which major changes are likely to occur is a critical first step in setting the time horizon for analysis. In some markets, like personal computers, the time horizon may be measured in months. In other markets, such as commercial aircraft, the time horizon to fundamental change stretches far off into the future.

Anticipating the pace of change in a market should be part and parcel of your study of demand trends, competitive developments, and so forth. However, you should also be thinking hard about the period of continuity for which the strategic proposal will be valid.

Flexibility of Commitment   By definition, a strategic proposal involves a commitment that is hard to reverse. But the flexibility or reversibility of proposals does vary. The less flexible the strategic commitment the further ahead you must look. For example, a consumer packaged-goods company may be able to introduce a new product on a limited basis, in test areas, thereby reducing the scale of the required initial investment. However, if a resource company is considering the development of a new mine, there are no half measures. The company will have to make the whole investment, and it may may not earn returns for several years. In such cases the time horizon for analysis is correspondingly extended.

Implementation Horizon   Some strategic ventures, like the mining example just mentioned and other major capital projects, require years of planning and construction to complete. In such cases these logistical realities determine the relevant period for environment analysis.

Setting a time horizon is more subtle for strategic initiatives that count on major organizational change to support them. Organizations have great inertia. If you want to be ahead of, or at least ready for, new developments, you have to look quite a distance down the road. In later chapters we develop the topics of strategic and organizational change and these will give you the base for making judgments about necessary and required time horizons from an implementation standpoint.

Defining the Right Time Horizon: The Jantzen Example   The Jantzen example calls for a base case analysis of a very successful business strategy. The crucial question is its sustainability—will the strategy continue to produce excellent results? The outcome of recent sales negotiations suggests that Jantzen's business environment is changing; customers are putting a new emphasis on price and competitors are meeting these demands. In this context, the time horizon for analysis is immediate. The changes are already under way that will create a substantially new set of environment conditions.

Minimizing the Risks of Focus

We have gone to some lengths to emphasize the importance of focus in your environment analysis. This makes for an efficient process and provides specific, in-depth results. It is important for you to recognize that these benefits are possible only at the risk of what we call *strategic myopia.* If your focus is too specific, you might miss the emergence of a new market opportunity, or the arrival of unconventional competition. Similarly, if you concentrate overly on a particular time horizon you may get blindsided by events that lie just beyond the limit.

The risks of focus can be reduced, however, by ensuring that your analysis is accompanied by continuous macroenvironment scanning, and that the analysis is recycled as it proceeds, to incorporate the redefinition, as necessary, of both the relevant environment and questions being addressed. With these precautions, the practical advantages of concentrated analysis far outweigh the risk and disadvantages of missing something.

Macroenvironment Scanning   A sensible hedge against the risks of focus is to maintain a concurrent awareness of the events and institutions surrounding the relevant business environment—what is called *macroenvironment scanning.* The chief differences between the focused environment analysis that we have been talking about and macroenvironment scanning are summarized in Table 4.1. Macroenvironment scanning is essentially an issue-seeking process. It is an on-going search for basic developments that may offer a firm brand-new opportunities or present an unconventional threat to its continuing performance.

A popular model for macroenvironment scanning is summarized by the acronym PEST, which stands for the basic variable categories in the model—Political, Economic, Social, and Technological trends. The aim in reviewing these trends is to identify broad forces and basic changes in the total environment of a business. A broadly based assessment is particularly useful when the uncertainty in the environment is very high and there is a need to create scenarios and unconventional new strategic options.[1] But you need to be careful here; the aim is to look wide, but avoid aimlessness. A useful approach is to take analytic expeditions that work outward from your defined business environment. Used this way, macroenvironment scanning and the PEST model become an extension of your basic strategy-environment analysis. The underlying guidelines are set by your understanding of your business strategy and its environment. From this

TABLE 4.1
Comparison of Focused Environment Analysis and Macroenvironment Scanning

	Key Characteristics	Primary Subjects	Output
Focused Environment Analysis	• Driven by strategic proposal • Relatively formal	• Analysis of fit with forces in defined environment	• Forecast of performance • Decision to proceed
Macro-environment Scanning	• Issue seeking • Continuous, informal process	• Fundamental social, economic, and technical trends	• Identify events of potential impact on the business

base you can screen the many events that occur on the fringe of the business environment and isolate those that have a potential impact on the business.

Identifying Market Intrusions   A second way to minimize the risks of focus is to keep your eyes open for newcomers into your industry. Trucks and aircraft have taken business that historically belonged to the railroads. Plastics have replaced wood, paper, and metals in numerous applications. The development of new technology is often the edge that allows outsiders to break into an industry and successfully penetrate its markets. You don't need incredible foresight to recognize these developments; you simply need to keep watch on patent registrations, technical reports, and products or processes already in use in other industries that may be applicable in your own situation. Given the time lags associated with truly novel commercial development and market diffusion, there will be enough time to respond, as long as a clear and imaginative view is taken of the potential of the innovation and the intentions of its sponsors.

Recycling   A third hedge against the risks of focus is to ensure that the analytic process stays open—that you are prepared to incorporate new information and to double back or recycle your work as the need arises. This proposition is easy to agree with in the abstract, but difficult to follow in practice. Recycling breaks the momentum of a proposal and may require substantial additional analysis. You may be reluctant, particularly in ambiguous situations, to go back a step, perhaps to the beginning, and redefine and reassess the situation. Fight this tendency or you will lose the important benefits of learning about new possibilities as the work develops.

Naturally, there is a limit to recycling. You must be careful to avoid the extreme of "analysis paralysis." At some point risks must be taken and decisions must be made. The art of good analysis is the ability to balance the need for additional study with the need to take action. You should be fully aware of this balance at all stages of your strategic work.

STEP 2: TEST THE STRATEGY-ENVIRONMENT LINKAGE

We now turn to the task of testing how well a strategic proposal addresses the opportunities, challenges, and timing requirements of the environment. To help organize this process we have classified environmental forces into four basic categories: demand, supply, competition, and government. The elements of this model are is portrayed in Figure 4.2. In the following sections we will review each of the environment categories and present several concepts that will help you to pursue your analysis. This is by no means an exhaustive review of environmental forces or of the analytic concepts that can be applied to them; such a review would take us well beyond the purpose and boundaries of this text. Rather, it is our intention to suggest some productive approaches that rely for their pursuit on your accumulated experience or further reading.

As the process of questioning and testing proceeds you will develop a better understanding of environment conditions and an accumulating evaluation of the strategy-environment fit. These may lead to an early conclusion that the strategic proposal is inadequate, in which case you should recycle the analysis, as indicated in Figure 4.1, to develop a better proposal that incorporates your findings.

FIGURE 4.2

Testing the Strategy- Environment Linkage

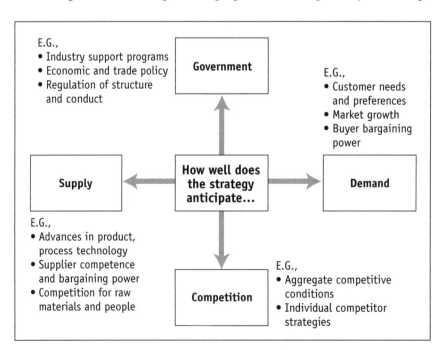

Demand

The test of the linkage of your proposal and and demand is whether it anticipates opportunities and creates advantages in the way that it addresses customer requirements and trends in the market. Is the strategy aimed at growing market segments? Does the strategy tap into new customer needs? In this process it is particularly important for you to gauge the degree to which a strategic proposal incorporates (1) the needs and preferences of current and potential customers; (2) the scale and timing of market development; and (3) the bargaining power of customers.

Needs and Preferences   It is surprising and discomforting to observe the degree to which companies will sometimes commit themselves to strategies without pinning down the fundamentals of anticipated demand. The literature on new product development is full of warnings on this account and of examples of setbacks in companies that ought to have known better, such as Coca Cola (the New Coke introduction) and Disney (the faltering start-up of EuroDisney).[2] The lesson is that you simply shouldn't feel comfortable unless you understand the links between your strategy and your intended customers.

Consider the strategic change that drove a turnaround at the Blockbuster Video chain. After several years of rapid growth, Blockbuster's sales and profitability faltered in 1995–96. Some analysts explained the slump by pointing to the increasing popularity of new technologies such as video on demand, but the real source of the problem was utterly prosaic. Customer service levels at Blockbuster had been sacrificed to the point where one in five shoppers went home empty-handed and many more left without the exact video that they wanted.[3] How could a company like Blockbuster underestimate the importance of having available the videos that customers wanted when they visited the store? It was partially out of arrogance, no doubt, but beneath this there was a strategy and profit model under which Blockbuster purchased tapes outright from the movie studios, making a fully adequate inventory a very expensive proposition. As a result, it had become commonplace at Blockbuster to manage dissatisfaction rather than to deal with the basic customer service issue; now that dissatisfaction was showing up in deteriorating performance. The habits of the past were so ingrained, moreover, that it took a new and forceful CEO to highlight the importance of customer service and to work out a solution to the problem. This was not easy; to support new higher service levels, Blockbuster had to completely overhaul its profit model. It did so by negotiating a new deal with the studios under which revenue-sharing arrangements were used to sharply reduce the fixed purchase cost of tapes. This made adequate inventories feasible, at the penalty, of course, of unit profit margins. But the result was an immediate improvement in business.

The problem in such instances is not that managers are unaware of the importance of customer needs and preferences. It is that other priorities get in the way. Blockbuster is a case in point. Another example is the belated recognition in 1998 by Levi Strauss & Co. that its basic North American blue jeans business was in trouble. Changing demographics and tastes had been leaving Levi's traditionally dominant jeans behind and creating opportunities for new competitors such as Tommy Hilfiger, Calvin Klein, The Gap, JNCO and others. But Levi was slow to take note, in good part because its design, marketing, and merchandising units operated quite autonomously, to the point, even, of working from separate office buildings.[4] Structure and politics were getting in the way of timely focus and market response. Levi ultimately moved to streamline its organization and get on with a push into new fashion concepts.

A major benefit of periodic strategic reviews is that they give you the opportunity to stand back and make sure that customer needs and preferences are being effectively addressed by your organization.

Scale and Timing of Market Development   The goals of a strategic proposal set out performance expectations. A critical test of these promises is whether the revenue projections are reasonably consistent with the anticipated scale and pace of market development. The uncertainties that you will need to address in this test will vary across the product market life cycle. In the early stages of the cycle, the major concern is timing: When and at what rate will the market develop? Later, with growth established, the key question is one of ultimate potential: Where is the ceiling? Even later, in maturity, the worry is vulnerability: How will substitutes affect future demand?

Timing is a particularly crucial issue in many strategic proposals. The questions that you will face are often not so much whether a market exists, but how fast it will develop (and what can be done to speed up the process). Consider the timing questions facing the sponsors and associated suppliers of the Mondex stored-value electronic cash card. Deployment of the card will require the development of a complex supporting infrastructure ranging from telecommunications devices to merchant participation. Behind this, the fundamental question, for everyone involved, is the rate of customer acceptance. Investing too much, too soon, would be an easy way to lose money. Moving too slowly, however, might well condemn your business and the product itself to a very long and difficult growth curve. In general, in strategic analysis you can make major contributions by going well beyond the absolutes of ultimate demand and pressing very hard on the issues of timing. They often turn out to be the critical uncertainties in a proposal.

Customer Bargaining Power   In consumer goods and services, customer buying power is an aggregate phenomenon, summarizing the collective ability and willingness of buyers to influence prices and volumes. A significant question in the analysis of the fit of a strategy with demand forces is whether the strategy properly anticipates the timing and degree of change in buying power that will occur as a result of industry disruptions, such as the advent of deregulation, or with time across product life cycles. In the case of the deregulation of the telecommunications industry in Canada, for example, the early strategic responses of the traditional regional monopoly members of the national Stentor alliance were overly cautious in nature and timing. Their responses reflected a serious underestimation of the speed with which customers would embrace new options and apply collective pressure for price and service improvements.

In industrial goods, demand is shaped more directly by the bargaining power of individual customers. For example, the auto makers usually have a high degree of bargaining power because (1) they buy goods in quantities that represent important volumes to their suppliers; (2) they have a choice of suppliers from which to buy; and (3) they have the capability, should they choose to exercise it, of integrating backward into production for themselves. As a consequence, the supplier firms in the industry are frequently caught in tough bargaining situations in which their customers have a distinct advantage. To counter such circumstances, suppliers build strategies to link their customers into their unique capabilities and to spread the risk of individual projects by maintaining a broad portfolio of contracts and customers.

There are, of course, many aspects of demand that you will need to consider as you review the prospects of your strategy. The key is to stay on track and stick to fundamental issues such as we have illustrated with the foregoing examples.

Supply

A further test of the linkage between your strategic ideas and the environment lies in the potential for advantage and disadvantage in supply conditions and trends. Consider, for example, the possibilities in the matching or mismatching of strategy with (1) technology, (2) supplier competence and bargaining power, and (3) competition for raw materials and people.

Technology   If your strategy anticipates developments in technology it might give you a head start on your rivals and an opportunity for industry leadership. The pioneer Internet bookseller Amazon.com, for example, capitalized rapidly on new possibilities in electronic commerce and took the leadership in this growing marketplace, much to the chagrin of conventional booksellers Barnes & Noble Inc. and Borders Group Inc. In seven years, Cisco Systems grew from a $70-million company to an $8-billion giant by capturing the lead in the provision of hardware for the Internet. On the other hand, if your strategies fail to anticipate and respond to technical change you might quickly become the laggard in the industry. Motorola, for example, underestimated the speed with which telecommunications technology would shift from analogue to digital networks and found themselves reliant on fast-fading analogue technology with very serious consequences for corporate performance and reputation. As in the estimation of demand forces, the issue with technology is often one of timing; it is critical that you keep your strategic reviews up to date on the pace of new developments.

Supplier Competence and Bargaining Power   Another area of potential strategic advantage or constraint that you need to check out is in the linkage of strategies to the competence and bargaining power of suppliers. The ability of strategies to create marketplace advantages, for example, will often depend on high levels of supplier competence. Retailers such as Home Depot and Canadian Tire are a case in point: their ability to deliver superior prices and in-stock reliability relies heavily on their programs to develop supplier competence, to the point of virtual integration through electronic data interchange. Their considerable bargaining power relative to most suppliers helps expedite the process of development and integration. When the shoe is on the other foot, however, supplier capabilities and bargaining power can be a significant problem. Wal-Mart's expansion in Brazil and Argentina, for example, has been delayed by both the reluctance and the limited competence of local suppliers and their superior bargaining power relative to the Wal-Mart start-up business.

If you face powerful suppliers that can influence the cost, quality, and delivery of essential inputs, you need to account for this in the development of your strategic proposal. Fabricators of steel products, for example, try to reduce their reliance on powerful raw steel suppliers by seeking product markets where they can incorporate value-added services in design and installation, and reduce their reliance on raw steel supplies.

Competition for Raw Materials and People   In many industries the most significant strategic opportunities lie in the ability to achieve an advantage in raw materials and people. You will need to be particularly careful in these instances to check that your strategic proposals have fully considered these possibilities. In resources, for example, the quantity and relative cost of gas, oil, timber rights, mineral deposits, and so forth go a long way towards defining the position and future possibilities for the companies in their respective industries. The critical strategic test in these industries lies in how well the businesses develop and sustain their raw materials positions. Consider two parallel situations in the nickel industry: Inco's investment in new capacity at Voisey's Bay, and Anaconda Nickel Inc.'s new mine developments in Australia. Analysts estimated that Anaconda's costs would be about one third of Inco's![5] If these estimates are

even approximately true, Anaconda has gained a huge advantage and put itself in a position to take market share from Inco and to do so at a profit.

In skill- and service-intensive industries, businesses vie to become the "best
company to work for." An advantage in people can readily be translated into
an advantage in the marketplace. Microsoft, ranked Number 7 in *Fortune*'s survey of the "One Hundred Best Companies in America to Work For,"[6] works at
least as hard to dominate the market for software engineers as it does to dominate the market for software products. Southwest Airlines, ranked Number 1
in the same survey, has translated its capacity to attract energetic and flexible people into a formidable advantage over more traditional airline competitors.

Competition

The test of the linkage of a strategic proposal and competition is in whether it
pursues competitive opportunities and offsets competitive challenges and vulnerabilities. Consider, for example, the development and appraisal of a strategy
relative to (1) aggregate competitive conditions and their impact on market attractiveness, and (2) the specific strategies of individual competitors.

Aggregate Competitive Conditions   You will need to check product market
entry strategies, in particular, against an assessment of the attractiveness of the
market as determined by aggregate competitive conditions. In this process,
Michael Porter's "five forces" model provides a useful vehicle to gauge rivalry and
the resulting attractiveness of industries and market segments.[7]

The five forces model examines a combination of competitive characteristics which influence the profit potential of an industry: (1) the threat of new entrants; (2) the bargaining power of suppliers; (3) the bargaining power of
customers; (4) the threat of substitute products or services; and (5) the rivalry
among current competitors. The collective strength of these forces determines
the ultimate profit potential of an industry, ranging from relatively intense
competition in industries like tires and steel, where firms have difficulty earning adequate returns, to relatively mild competition in industries such as soft
drinks and toiletries, where firms can earn above-average returns. The application
of this model is particularly useful in assessing the attractiveness of potential
product markets.

Consider the industry level opportunities and obstacles faced by a privately
held manufacturer of plastic drainage products. The company's early growth had
been based on an innovative application of extrusion technology to the fabrication of corrugated plastic pipe for agricultural and industrial drainage. In
may applications the new plastic pipe provided significant advantages in cost and
ease of installation over existing clay, steel, and concrete products. After a very
profitable 10-year period, however, a number of changes in the industry were

squeezing growth and profitability. Product and process technologies for existing applications had matured and were readily available to competitors and to new entrants. Large installation contractors were bargaining successfully for very significant price and delivery concessions. Resin suppliers had consolidated and accumulated significant bargaining power relative to users. And substitute product producers in steel and concrete had redesigned their product lines to compete vigorously with the plastic contender. Together these forces were creating an unattractive market. The company's response, after an appreciable delay in recognizing what was happening, was to shift its product market focus to very large-diameter applications that had not been developed because of technical obstacles, and to invest heavily in a risky process development program. As it turned out, the development efforts were successful and the resulting proprietary technology allowed the company to repeat its earlier success, only now in a new and, for a time at least, more attractive industry segment.

Individual Competitor Strategies   In many markets competition boils down to a handful of readily identifiable competitors. In these situations it is imperative for you to look at the competitors individually, study their strategies, and determine the potential impacts on your strategic intentions. More specifically you should be trying to determine (1) how capable each competitor is, and how steadfast it will be in pursuing its strategic course; (2) how your strategic proposal might affect the competitor's prospects; and (3) how motivated and capable each competitor is to react to your strategic initiative, and how it might go about doing so. These results, in turn, will condition your expectations for your own strategic proposal.

At times, the strategies of close competitors are reasonably easy to figure out. Monsanto has long been developing its capabilities in the growing crop biotechnology industry. When rival Dupont spent nearly $3 billion in 1997 on acquisitions and partnerships in the industry, its underlying strategy was quite apparent. Dupont was intent on weaving together a formidable competitive position by integrating the core activities of crop biotechnology from basic science to farm distribution. Monsanto had little choice but to respond in kind if it intended to be a long-run contender in the industry. Accordingly, a year later Monsanto was in the process of bolstering its position through over $5 billion in acquisitions including DeKalb Genetics Corp., Delta and Pine Land, and Cargill Inc.'s international seed operations.

At other times it is more difficult to pin down what your competitors are up to. Consider the probable consternation of Coke when Pepsico announced that it intended to purchase the Tropicana Juice company. Coke and Pepsi, of course, were traditional rivals in soft drinks and each knew virtually every step and misstep the other was involved in or had planned in this marketplace. In the orange juice industry Coke had long owned the Minute Maid brand. Minute Maid had a dominant position in the frozen concentrate segment of the industry and was making inroads into the chilled juice segment. Tropicana was the dominant brand in chilled juice and would give any acquiring firm a strong starting position. But the orange juice industry's market was not a particularly attractive one; profit margins were far lower than Pepsi's soft drink and snack food businesses and required entirely different purchasing, manufacturing, and distribution activities. What was Pepsi up to? What were the implications for Minute Maid? Would Pepsi be resolute or could it be pushed back? These were difficult questions to answer given that the prospects of the Tropicana investment, in the words of one analyst, were "not a layup by any means."[8]

These examples underline a key point. However obvious or obscure the situation, it is only at your peril that you ignore or underestimate competitors or the potential for competition. Knowing your competitors, like knowing your customers, is a central law of survival and success.

Government

Government involvement is a pervasive aspect of the business environment. Whether we like it or not, governments play many roles—from framing and implementing the basic legal framework for business conduct, to establishing taxes, incentives, and supports, to being customers and even competitors, and on and on. The scope and importance of government activity in the economy is enormous, creating a complex context of opportunities and constraints for businesses. It is vitally important that you train a clear eye on these realities as you create and test strategic proposals. Consider, for example, the importance for strategy of correctly anticipating (1) government support, (2) changing trade policy, and (3) regulatory compliance.

Government Support   Many businesses and industries operate with a level of government support that goes well beyond that normally available to everyone. Some of this support is direct, for example, in grants and subsidies for research or plant location. Some is indirect, for example, in preferential legislation that provides protection from foreign competition. You need to carefully weigh your strategy in terms of its ability to create advantage from government support and to offset any potential changes in support activities. Some film production companies, for example, seek cost advantages by working in locations where generous government incentives are available. And pharmaceutical companies throughout the world use their considerable research and development spending as a bargaining chip in lobbying for the maintenance of patent protection.

Some companies leverage their strategies on close government ties. Consider the way in which Bombardier, for example, has used its considerable skills in government relations to help build its various businesses. Bombardier's market entry and expansion activities have often been driven by opportunities to assist governments who have become embroiled in troubled transport and aerospace facilities. Some examples are the acquisition of rail transit and rolling-stock assets in Canada and Mexico respectively, and of aircraft assets in Canada and Ireland. In these and other circumstances, Bombardier has demonstrated a capacity to acquire technology and plant facilities on advantageous terms, and to integrate these advantages into its total operations. On another front, Bombardier has also been very aggressive and skilful in developing a government customer base for its transportation projects. The company's willingness to target government and its effectiveness in sorting its way through complex economic and political considerations has given it significant advantages over more conventional competitors.

Changes in Trade Policy   In the past 20 years or so, governments have been backing away from regulation and protectionism. Overall, the aim is to improve economic efficiency by increasing the opportunities open to businesses and with this, the competition that they face. As deregulation and trade liberalization proceed, albeit in fits and starts at times, it is crucially important that you develop strategies that anticipate the freedoms created by the changing circumstances and the challenges of new competition.

Consider, for example, how aggressive and successful Air Canada has been in developing the opportunities created by the 1995 Open Skies agreement between Canada and the United States. This agreement substantially deregulated cross-border air travel, with the exception of a three-year phase-in period applying to Montreal, Toronto, and Vancouver. There was a fear at the time that even with the phase-in period the giant U.S. airlines would soon dominate the market. But Air Canada seized the opportunity instead and rapidly increased service, leveraging particularly on its protected Toronto hub and deploying a fleet of new, flexible Bombardier Regional Jets. By 1998, when Toronto airport was opened to all comers, Air Canada was flying almost as many cross-border flights as all the U.S. airlines combined. At the same time, Air Canada had also far outpaced rival Canadian Airlines whose own expansion had been limited by financial and fleet difficulties. Air Canada's strategy to capitalize on open skies had won the day, big time.

Regulatory Compliance   The matter of compliance is often straightforward—the rules are clear and the actions anticipated in your strategic proposal either comply or they don't. At times, however, compliance is not nearly so easy as it sounds. Some policies are vague, requiring judgments by the business, regulatory authorities, or even in the courts. Some policies are administered inconsistently, and some are changed in midstream. In these murkier circumstances you will need to take great care in identifying the regulatory sensitivities in your strategic plans and in working out an action plan to deal with them.

Consider the circumstances of McDonald's in China. Its 34 Beijing restaurants have paid an average of 31 fees each to municipal authorities, of which only 14 are legal, the balance being levied arbitrarily by various and sundry local offices and officials to serve their particular needs.[9] These extra fees amounted to about $10 000 per year per restaurant. The problems for McDonald's, and for others investing in the Beijing area, were those of cost, of course, but more importantly, the uncertainty of future costs, if such a regime of unpublished and haphazard fees were to continue. There was not much that foreign investors in Beijing could actually do except to reflect the uncertainties in their investment decisions and this, in fact, was being cited as one cause for lower investment rates in Beijing as compared with other major Chinese cities. There is ample warning for you to carefully monitor the regulatory context and sensitivity of your strategies.

Testing the Strategy-Environment Linkage: The Jantzen Example So how well does Jantzen's existing strategy fit its environment? The answer, unfortunately, is not very well at all. The strategy does not fit with the environment of maturing demand and competition. The inconsistencies are so great, in fact, that even with this first set of qualitative tests it is clear that a complete reformulation of Jantzen's business strategy is badly overdue.

A major problem facing Jantzen was the changing nature of market requirements for its component product. In earlier years its PC manufacturer customers were very receptive to the custom design support and technical liaison that Jantzen provided so well. Now, these same manufacturers were facing fierce competition in their own markets and looking for ways to reduce their product costs. One route was to standardize components, develop alternative suppliers, and press for low prices. This was diluting Jantzen's competitive edge in custom design and its traditional strength in customer relationships, since engineers were now being displaced on buying teams by purchasing and manufacturing executives. And with the standardization of products increasing, independent distributors, which Jantzen had chosen largely to ignore, were starting to take a greater position in the market by servicing the many smaller, local, PC assemblers.

As if demand shifts weren't enough, a number of well-qualified competitors were now operating in the market. These competitors had mastered the basic technology, erasing much of Jantzen's competitive lead. Within the established technology, however, there were still rapid changes in product speed and capacity, which left competitors leapfrogging each other to deliver the best performance for a price. In spite of the pace of product change, some of the new competitors had chosen to operate as designers and assemblers and rely quite heavily on a rapidly developing and very competitive, global sub-component supply industry. These competitors had been foremost in cutting prices in recent months. A further and quite disturbing development for Jantzen were the announced plans of two of the largest PC manufacturers, who had previously produced the component solely to meet a portion of their own needs, to enter the open market as merchant suppliers.

Jantzen's strategy was being eclipsed by demand and competitive developments. There might be room in the industry for it to continue as a specialist supplier, but this would cap its ability to grow. If Jantzen wants to grow it has to radically change its value proposition and core activities to conform with new industry realities. At this point of analysis it would be appropriate to recycle and create a new strategy for the company.

First Check for Fit or Recycle

You have now completed an initial assessment of how well your strategic proposal anticipates and addresses demand, supply, competition, and government. If some serious questions have come up in the course of this analysis, now is the time to stop and reshape the proposal or build a substantially new proposal that incorporates the accumulated understanding of the environment. There is nothing to be gained from spending more time on a strategic proposal that obviously doesn't fit with the environment. On the other hand, if the proposal seems reasonable in most respects (not perfect, because perfect doesn't happen in such complex considerations) the analysis should move on to a forecast of performance to see if the proposal will meet its goals.

STEP 3: FORECAST PERFORMANCE

As you move to forecasting the expected performance of your strategic proposal, it is important to recall a beginning assumption in the strategy-environment analysis—that the strategic proposal, by and large, will be implemented as planned. In other words, you are assuming that the business has the will and the capabilities to put the strategy into place. These additional issues of will and capability come later in the drill, after there is some assurance that you are working with a proposal that suits the environmental realities. It would be an obvious waste of time to go into the other considerations if the proposal can't pass this first test!

The goals incorporated in the strategic proposal provide a useful reference point for the performance forecast. The question that you want to answer is whether the strategic proposal, implemented as planned, will meet these goals.

By this stage in the analysis you will have already weeded out the proposals that clearly do not fit with the environment. Now, you must focus on those that remain. Work systematically through the strategic goals for each proposal (for example, the revenue, cost, return, and investment goals) and use what you have learned about the environment to draw conclusions about the likelihood of achieving them.

While this is being done it is useful to identify and note the primary risks entailed. These points of risk are helpful to focus the immediate analysis as well as the subsequent comparison of the current proposal with competing alternatives. We will illustrate the process with respect to the two most tangible goal dimensions: revenues and costs.

The strategic goals for revenue growth and their underlying components of price and unit volume need to be evaluated in the light of the way that the strategic proposal addresses expected developments in the environment. Is the strategy powerful enough to deliver the promise? Watch out for questionable assumptions about market growth and about the impact of competitive activity. A fault that we often see in strategic proposals in large companies is overly ambitious revenue goals, which are made without sufficient thought or, more deviously, are biased to justify the project that is being proposed. Were the Jantzen strategy pushed to this point the issue would be whether the company could sustain prices and increase volumes at over 20 percent in the next few years. While the overall *growth* in demand for PCs might support this expectation, the changing *nature* of demand has diluted Jantzen's value proposition and the advent of aggressive competition suggests severe pricing pressures in the market.

Cost performance goals require just as critical an eye. First you want to ensure that the projected operating costs incorporate anticipated supply developments and the possibilities of government regulatory or tax action. This is relatively straightforward. A more difficult task is to evaluate the cost goals that hinge on competitive conditions. What are the promotional costs, for example, that will be required to introduce a new product? And further, what is the possibility of competitively induced cost changes as time goes by in such areas as distribution margins, credit allowances, transportation arrangements, advertising and promotion spending, and so on?

As you continue to test performance forecasts against strategic goals, you may begin to question the goals or the other supporting elements of the strategic proposal. Here again it is time to recycle the proposal using the new information to revise the strategy. This time try to use the analysis to improve the proposal; abandonment should come only after some good creative effort has failed to address your concerns.

STEP 4: RANK AGAINST OTHER PROPOSALS

At this point the strategic proposal is considered to be compatible with the environment. Subject to some understood risks, it is expected to achieve its goals. The only question before going on to other steps of the Diamond-E drill is whether it is competitive with other proposals you are considering. A definitive answer is impossible until the whole drill has been completed, but a preliminary screen can weed out proposals that promise less or have higher risks, or in some other way are not competitive with others in the running. If the proposal is clearly not competitive then shift your attention to the superior options. Otherwise, it is time to move on and examine the strategy-resource linkage.

SUMMARY

This chapter has presented the basic steps for analyzing the links between strategy and environment. The early priority in this process is to focus the analysis, and we demonstrated the utility of performance assessment, the strategic proposal, and the business profit model in pursuing this task. We acknowledged the potential risks of overfocusing the analysis, but argued that there are sufficient safeguards in a careful process of analysis that the merits of focus well exceed the risks involved.

The next step of analysis is to examine the substance of the strategic proposal in the light of current and anticipated demand, supply, competition, and government policy. For demonstrably poor fits we suggested developing a more attractive proposal that incorporated the insights gained in the analysis.

The next step is to forecast the performance of the strategic proposal. If the forecast turns out to be consistent with the strategy's goals, the next steps are to compare it with alternatives and then move on to further stages of the Diamond-E drill. If the forecast is not consistent with its goals, the remedy, again, is to recycle and improve the proposition.

Now, armed with a proposal that fits with the environment, we turn our attention to its implementation. And the first topic to address is whether the resources needed to support the proposal are available or can be readily acquired or developed by the business.

NOTES

1. For an elaboration of this theme, see Hugh Courtney, Jane Kirkland, and Patrick Viguerie, "Strategy Under Uncertainty," *Harvard Business Review,* vol. 75 (November–December 1997), pp. 67–79.

2. For an instructive example of reading demand in high technology markets, see Benham Tabrizi and Rick Walleigh, "Defining Next-Generation Products: An Inside Look," *Harvard Business Review,* vol. 75 (November–December 1997), pp. 116–124.

3. "How Blockbuster Changed the Rules," *Time,* August 3, 1998.

4. "Levi's Decides It's Time to 'Break Rules'," *Wall Street Journal,* August 4, 1998.

5. "New Rival Sees Trouble for Inco," *Globe and Mail,* May 28, 1998.

6. "100 Best Companies to Work for in America," *Fortune,* January 12, 1998.

7. Michael E. Porter, "How Competitive Forces Shape Strategy," *Harvard Business Review,* vol. 57 (March–April 1979).

8. "Storming the OJ Wars, Pepsi to Buy Tropicana," *Wall Street Journal,* July 21, 1998.

9. "In China, McDonald's Pays at Every Turn," *Wall Street Journal,* September 5, 1997.

ADDITIONAL READINGS

BOWER, JOSEPH L. AND CLAYTON M. CHRISTENSON, "Disruptive Technologies: Catching the Wave," *Harvard Business Review,* vol. 73 (January–February 1995).

PORTER, MICHAEL E., *Competitive Strategy: Techniques for Analyzing Industries and Competitors.* New York: Free Press, 1985.

RESOURCE ANALYSIS: THE STRATEGY-RESOURCE LINKAGE

If you have worked through the analysis outlined in the previous chapter, you now have a strategic proposal that fits well with the external environment. Your analysis has shown that the proposal is likely to generate the kind of results that you want—if you can implement it!

The first implementation questions, which are addressed in this chapter, have to do with resources. What resources will you need to implement the proposal? What gaps are there between the resources required by the proposal and the resources that your business has on hand or readily available? What are the possibilities of closing the most important gaps? If the gaps are modest, or can be bridged at acceptable cost and risk, you can move to further steps of the Diamond-E drill. If the gaps are sizeable, however, and the risks of closing them are high, you will need to recycle to develop a more viable proposition.

This chapter discusses the nature and role of resources in the strategic process and sets out an analytic process to deal with the questions implicit in the strategy-resource linkage in the Diamond-E framework.

THE NATURE OF RESOURCES

Resources provide your business with the potential to act. To implement a strategic proposal you will need to draw on financial resources for the required investment, operating resources to supply the product or service, marketing resources for promotion and sales, and so on. In Table 5.1 we have classified the many and varied resources that you might have to refer to as you consider implementation and we have added some examples of particular resources in each category.

There are three important points to be made about the nature of resources as they relate to strategic choice. The first is that the adequacy of a resource is relative to the demands of your strategic proposal. Absolutes in terms of size or depth or scope may or may not be important. Chrysler, for example, was a

TABLE 5.1
Resource Categories and Examples

1. Marketing

• Scale • Market share • Brands • Product distinctiveness, reputation, and installed base • Distribution network • Sales force • Trade and customer relationships • Patents, copyrights

2. Operations

• Access to low-cost inputs • Supplier relationships • Plant costs, capacity, efficiency, and flexibility • Proprietary process, information technology, and know-how • Logistics reliability and efficiency • Quality reputation • Location

3. Development

• Expertise in product and process development • Scale of facilities, efforts • Pipeline of projects, products • Technology partnerships and agreements • Regulatory relationships • Links to scientific community

4. Financial

• Performance • Scale • Cash flow • Capacity to raise capital • Cost of capital • Investor (owner) expectations • Banking and investor relations • Resilience to cycles, shocks

5. Human Resources

• Depth, experience, skills, and flexibility of management, professional staff, and work force • Commitment, loyalty, morale • Positive relationships with unions, staff associations

6. Corporate Reputation

• Reputation of the business as a corporate citizen, employer, partner in alliances and joint ventures, competitor, acquiring firm • Relationships with business community, regulatory authorities, government agencies, and politicians

very large firm with very significant marketing, development, and financial resources, but in management's judgment these were insufficient to implement a strategy aimed at global scope, setting the stage for a merger with Daimler Benz. This suggests a caution about some approaches to strategic analysis that start from an absolute or internally referenced review of resources (such as the strengths and weaknesses component of a SWOT analysis—strengths, weaknesses, opportunities, and threats). You need to cast resources in the context of their intended utilization before they can be said to be adequate or otherwise.

A second noteworthy characteristic is that certain resources are more or less easy to augment or adapt to meet the requirements of a proposal. If plant capacity is an issue, for example, it may be fairly simple to reallocate it, or to expand as necessary through investment. But if critical work force skills are the issue, it may take substantial time to hire and train the needed people and in some circumstances this may not be a practical possibility at all. Thus, as your analysis proceeds and you perceive gaps, you will have to be sensitive to the particular issues of expanding the specific resource to meet the strategic needs.

A final notable characteristic is that particular resources are more or less transferable to new applications. A brand name might easily transfer to a new product line. But management skills developed in a particular market, say Canada, may not easily transfer into, say, Mexico. Again, the caution is to be sensitive to the potential issues of transferring what are otherwise good and solid resources to your particular proposal.

Other Characterizations of Resources

We have characterized resources in specific terms to keep the analysis of your strategic proposal as tangible and as operational as possible. In wider ranging discussions about the future direction of your business, however, such as in the development of missions, visions, and very broad strategic thrusts, you may find it useful to work with more broadly based conceptions of resources. Here are three possibilities for you to consider—presented in the chronological order in which they have appeared in the strategy literature.

In the late 1950s Selznick[1] and Ansoff[2] used the term *distinctive competence* to highlight the core activities that a business can perform better than its competitors. Thus, Dow Chemical might be said to have a distinctive competence in the low-cost production of commodity chemicals. The implications of this concept for strategy formulation are clear cut, in that distinctive competences are, in effect, competitive advantages. In their strategies, businesses should seek to exploit their distinctive competences and to avoid initiatives which hold no relationship to them.

In the early 1970s Wrigley[3] introduced the term *core skills* to describe the collective skills accumulated by a management or professional team as they worked together over time in a common pursuit. Thus, Merck might be said to have developed core skills in the process of bringing a drug product from discovery through commercialization. The core skills possessed by businesses represent potentially valuable resources in that they are not easy to develop—and hence hard for competitors to copy. The implications for strategy are that a business ought carefully to identify and nourish its core skills and use them as reference points in creating or evaluating new initiatives.

In the 1990s Prahalad and Hamel[4] further developed the notion of competing on the basis of unique resources by introducing the concept of *core competences*. Core competences are the skills possessed by corporations that underlie a whole range of products and business units, such as miniaturization in the case of Sony and materials coating in the case of 3M. Although the various resource concepts are now becoming somewhat redundant, the particular spins that the authors put on them can add value to your analysis. Thus, core competences, conceived of as corporate resources, provide a focal point for strategy at the corporate level and give direction to corporate management in the integration of the efforts of the various parts of the corporation.

The advantages of summary conceptions of resources, such as those of distinctive competence, core skills, and core competence, lie in the facility they provide for informal and open-ended explorations of strategic direction. We find the notion of distinctive competence, in particular, a quick and easy reference point in creating and sorting through ideas and in raising questions for subsequent, more detailed analysis. The disadvantages of these concepts, however, lies in their high level of abstraction, which creates difficulties pinning down whether they really do exist in a particular business and subsequently in testing the validity of specific strategic ideas. We are aware, for example, of businesses that have become very frustrated trying to pin down their core competences and in this respect Collis and Montgomery criticize the search for core competences as too often becoming "a feel good exercise that no one fails."[5] Perhaps more dangerously, these concepts might build a false confidence that they provide a sufficient basis for actual decisions, and lead to ignoring or slighting the many specific resources that are critical to any undertaking.

Our advice is simply to proceed with an understanding that there are natural phases of exploration and analysis. In early exploratory work the broad concepts are useful. But as the analysis proceeds it is critically important that you move to an operational definition of your strategic proposal and to the consideration of specific, tangible resource requirements.

THE DUAL ROLE OF RESOURCES

Resources both constrain and drive strategy. Inadequate resources may prevent you from implementing strategic proposals that otherwise make sense in light of the opportunities and challenges in your firm's external environment. Powerful resources may drive strategy if they represent a potential for competitive advantage that can be exploited with the right strategic approach.

The Constraining Role of Resources

Most managers are all too familiar with the powerful role that resources can play in constraining strategy. Often, a strategic proposal promises to take the business into growing markets with good profit potential, but a look at resources suggests that the firm does not really have the resources that it needs to implement it. How long would it take to develop or acquire the needed resources? Or is it possible to modify the strategy to take advantage of the resources that are available? On one hand, you don't want to overstretch your resources; on the other, you can't afford to enter too late into the new market, or risk making customer promises that you cannot meet.

Consider the situation facing Steve Jobs when he reassumed control of Apple Computer in 1997. Apple's resources had been ravished by years of unsettled management—among other things, finances were stretched, market share was down to around three percent, many program developers had stopped producing for the Apple line, and customers were questioning the credibility of the business as an ongoing proposition. In the face of this, Apple was compounding its problems by stretching its remaining resources across 15 different computer products. With an understanding that Apple would surely fail if it continued to try to operate beyond its resource constraints, Jobs pressed for simplification of the product line to focus on just two market categories and four new products. This move had its own risks as Jobs acknowledged: "We're the last company left that can bet a company on a new idea—this is Apple's future."[6] But these were necessary risks given the company's need to work within its resource limitations.

The Driving Role of Resources

On the other hand, resources can be an extremely important driving force, underlying the creation of new strategic proposals. Even in the case of Apple Computer, the company's powerful G3 microprocessor and loyal (if dwindling) customer base provided the seeds for the first products of the turnaround endeavour—the Power Mac G3 and PowerBook G3 for the professional market and the iMac for the consumer market.

Further, strategy may be driven by attempts to build and reinforce a resource advantage. First mover advantages may disappear if they are not pursued to their limit. Consider the case of Amazon.com. As an early entrant into on-line book sales, by 1998 Amazon.com had 2.5 million customers worldwide and sales projected to $350 million. In the face of new, look-alike competitors, Amazon.com's customer list was a valuable resource, but only if it was developed and protected. The company could not stand still. Whatever its ambitions, from a strategic standpoint Amazon.com had to continue to press for growth in books, in product lines such as CDs and airline tickets, and in any other ways that would add utility to its customers. Otherwise the resource represented by its leading customer list would dissipate and with this, Amazon.com's fortunes.

As you consider resource-pushed strategies it is vitally important not to lose sight of your customers. The trick is to identify, develop, and take advantage of your unique resources, without getting too inwardly focused. You may, for example, conceive an extremely innovative strategic proposal built on a unique resource, but you must ensure that this does not lead you to develop products or services that customers simply don't care about. For example, the New Product Showcase and Learning Center in Ithaca, New York, has a library of thousands of failed products launched by companies that thought it would be all too easy to extend a product line, or transfer a brand name, or otherwise try to leverage off existing resources.[7]

RESOURCE ANALYSIS

We now turn to the process of testing your strategic proposal against your firm's resources. The logical flow of this process is presented in Figure 5.1. In this process we concentrate on the constraining role of resources because this phase of the Diamond-E drill ultimately boils down to whether you have, or can develop, the resources needed to support your strategic proposal. If the immediate answer is no, you may turn to an examination of your existing resource base for inspiration regarding new strategic ideas, but any resulting proposal will still have to be re-cycled through the Diamond-E drill. The fact that a particular proposal was in-spired by the identification of a unique resource is no guarantee that the business will have the full set of resources required for its successful implementation.

The process outlined in Figure 5.1 takes you through three phases of analy-sis to (1) determine the resource requirements of the strategic proposal, (2) iden-tify gaps between the required and available resources, and (3) evaluate the

FIGURE 5.1

Resource Analysis

Step 1: Identify Resource Requirements
Work from the strategic proposal to clarify and project the resources required for implementation and ongoing success. Prepare at a level of detail that will facilitate analysis and management action.

GENERATE NEW STRATEGIC PROPOSAL(S)

Step 2: Test the Strategy-Resource Linkage
Compare the resource requirements with the counterpart resources in the business or readily available to it. Identify current and anticipated gaps between the two. For serious misfits recycle to develop a more attractive proposal.

Recycle

Step 3: Develop Gap-Closing Analysis
Assess the feasibility of closing any material gaps. If the costs, chances of success, and consequences of failure are acceptable, carry the proposal forward. If not, recycle to develop a more attractive proposal.

Recycle

Step 4: Move to Next Step in Diamond-E Drill
Assess the strategy-management preference linkage.

risks associated with closing the gaps. There are two subsidiary formats that you will find helpful in working through the analytic process. The first format, presented in Table 5.2, focuses on the use of the proposed strategy to identify and describe the relevant resource considerations. The second format, which is intended for concurrent use and ultimately as a summary document, is illustrated in Table 5.3. It helps you to highlight the resource categories in which there are going to be bottlenecks and your assessment of the likelihood of solving the problem.

STEP 1: IDENTIFY RESOURCE REQUIREMENTS

The starting point for your analysis is to determine the resources that are most critical to the successful implementation of your strategic proposal. To facilitate this, key on the strategic proposal and work back to the various resource areas in a systematic way. In particular, focus on the elements of your strategic proposal that represent a change from the status quo. If Jantzen Technologies, the personal computer component supplier described in Chapter 4, needs to begin to compete on price, for example, Harry Jantzen should focus on the resource

TABLE 5.2
Resource Analysis by Strategy Component

Strategic Proposal	Required	Available	Gaps	Risks
Goals	What are the most critical resources required by the goals of the strategic proposal (e.g., for growth, risk, market dominance); what are the gaps between these requirements and available resources; and what are the risks and consequences of not being able to close these gaps in a timely way?			
Product/Market Focus	What are the most critical resources required by the product market focus of the strategic proposal (e.g., for a specific market focus, diversification); what are the gaps between these requirements and available resources; and what are the risks and consequences of not being able to close these gaps in a timely way?			
Value Proposition	What are the most critical resources required by the value proposition of the strategic proposal (e.g., for price, features, execution); what are the gaps between these requirements and available resources; and what are the risks and consequences of not being able to close these gaps in a timely way?			
Core Activities	What are the most critical resources required by the core activities of the strategic proposal (e.g., for activities to internalize, degree of integration); what are the gaps between these requirements and observed resources; and what are the risks and consequences of not being able to close these gaps in a timely way?			

implications of that particular change. He will, for instance, need a marketing system tuned to the needs of an increasingly commodity-like product, product designers with an ability to create products that are simple to manufacture, manufacturing managers and facilities suited to longer runs of standardized products, demanding purchasing agents, and so on.

Some resource requirements are reasonably easy to predict. The financial requirements for a strategic proposal, for example, can be worked out as a matter of straightforward logic from the substance and performance forecasts of the proposal. When it comes to qualitative resources and particularly those of management skills, however, the resource requirements may be harder to pin down. In its early steps to enter South American markets, for example, Wal-Mart seemed to assume that the required leadership skills would be largely the same as those in the United States, making the requirements essentially a quantitative matter. This was far from the truth, however, as evidenced by Wal-Mart's early difficulties in these markets.[8] Wal-Mart's response was to the point, including, for them, the unprecedented step in hiring a senior manager from outside the firm to lead its international operations. The caution here is to be very careful about qualitative resource requirements because it is all too easy to assume that new requirements are just an extension of old requirements. This is where the quality of your understanding of your strategy and its environment linkages really comes under test.

Finally, as a matter of focus, concentrate your work on the resources that seem most critical to the execution of the strategy. The key to this is to under-

TABLE 5.3
Resource Analysis by Resource Category

Resource Category	Required Resources	Available Resources	Major Gaps	Gap-Closing Analysis
Marketing				
Operations				
Development				
Financial				
Human Resources				
Reputation				
Other				

stand what is unique about your strategy and, in particular, what competitive advantage it seeks to create or exploit. A strategy based on superior product features, for example, pushes you immediately to focus on the required development and commercialization resources.

STEP 2: TEST THE STRATEGY-RESOURCE LINKAGE

Once you have identified the most critical resources for implementing your strategic proposal, it should not take long to match them against the firm's existing resources. The advantage of determining the required resources first is that you now have a list that allows you to examine your existing resources in a focused way, and to avoid a "laundry list" approach. You know the resources that you need. The first task is to determine whether you have them, or can readily develop them. The second is to clarify the gaps that remain. If these gaps are truly formidable, it makes sense to drop the proposal and recycle the analysis to generate better ideas. If there is some hope, however, that extraordinary action might address the gaps, you pass to a third phase for an analysis of the practicality of the correction and risks involved. The following paragraphs provide some examples of linking strategy to resource requirements and availabilities in selected resource categories.

Marketing Resources   IBP, the giant U.S. meat processor, built its business by focusing on low-cost processing of cattle and hogs and the sale of a boxed product for further finishing and presentation at the retail level. By the early 1990s, however, competitors had imitated many of IBP's processing efficiencies and had moved further into such areas as branded, packaged, consumer-ready meat products. A similar move by IBP into consumer-ready products, however, would require significant marketing resources to handle product development, branding, pricing, and promotion, to build reputation and relationships in this area with the retail trade, and to deal with the complex distribution requirements. Given its commodity product history, IBP was very thin on these resources; the gaps amounted to starting from scratch in a new business area. At the time, IBP chose to keep to its traditional strategic focus. But the accumulating pressures of consumer, trade, and competitor trends over the next few years meant that IBP had ultimately to adapt its strategy and to address the resource issues. In 1997, the company announced a line of consumer-friendly beef and pork cuts and several significant acquisitions that, among other things, would provide scale and expertise in the new business area.[9]

Operations Resources   As the aircraft industry moved into a period of surging demand in the mid 1990s, Boeing adopted an aggressive strategy of maintaining share in the face of growing price and delivery pressure from the major airlines and the increasing capabilities of its key competitor, Airbus Industrie. New orders were booked at an unprecedented pace, which, if filled would require the company to double its production output in two years. Not a big deal you might think, for a progressive aerospace company. The problem, however, as *Fortune* reported it, was that, "Boeing executives have known for years—for decades even—that their factories were inefficient, their supply chains tangled, their computer systems outmoded. Ever since the 1970s they have tried, in a piecemeal fashion, to fix these problems. But they never took the issues seriously."[10] The Boeing culture was one of excellence in design and the tailoring of design to individual customers. In this, the urgency for simplification and efficiency in manufacturing was difficult to grasp. The result was a serious strategy-resource mismatch. Boeing's plants were overwhelmed to the point that they were actually shut down for a month to try to recover order and in the result Boeing absorbed losses estimated at $3 billion in 1998 and still counting, and a serious loss of credibility with customers and investors. It is quite possible that Boeing didn't have much choice on the strategic front—giving up share and follow-on business would probably have been prohibitively expensive. But management's insensitivity over time to the resource implications of foreseeable changes in environment and strategy surely cost the company dearly.

Financial Resources Balancing the requirements of strategic ambitions against the financial capacity of the business is a critical senior management responsibility. Consider the following contrasting examples.

After funding research on its Iridium satellite system for several years, Motorola, in the early 1990s, was faced with increasingly large funding requirements. The system, scheduled for start-up in the late 1990s, was to consist of a network of 88 satellites which would allow users to communicate, wirelessly, wherever they were on earth. Rather than change its strategic thrust or unduly stretch its resources, Motorola decided to bring in outside partners to help finance and develop the system. In 1998, when the Iridium network was launched, Motorola held an 18 percent interest in the business and was looking forward to the returns from its efforts. Motorola's steps in the case were not unusual; in the past decade many companies, faced with resource demands that they cannot meet, or unwilling to put too many eggs in one basket, have decided to form alliances with firms that can bring needed resources.

The perils of stretching your financial capacity to satisfy ambitious strategic goals are illustrated by the commitment of John Labatt Limited, the Canadian brewer, of $720 million in July 1994, to the purchase of 22 percent of the Mexican brewer FEMSA Cerveza. Whatever the strategic merit of the investment, the $720 million exposed about 65 percent of Labatt's net worth to a market and currency of questionable stability. Moreover, Labatt chose not to hedge the investment, probably because of the high costs of such a move, given that Mexican short-term interest rates were running at about 18 percent. In the event only five months later the Mexican economy fell into crisis, the peso plunged and Labatt was stuck with an major investment that had just lost half its Canadian dollar value. If Labatt had been a multi-billion dollar corporation this might have been written off as a regrettable but affordable loss. But such was its magnitude relative to Labatt's financial base that it triggered a takeover battle in which Labatt was ultimately purchased by the Belgian company, Interbrew.

Human Resources Through the 1990s traditional retail banks nearly everywhere were trying to grasp and respond to the new competitive possibilities being created by information technology and liberalizing regulation. Together these forces were reducing barriers to entry and threatening decades of orderly competition based on physical branches and face-to-face personal service. The various strategic responses open to the retail banks, which ranged across employing the new technology to reinforce their existing operations, to adding on services such as ATM, telephone, and personal computer access, to the creation of entirely new banking formats, had one thing in common—a requirement for attitudes and skills that were quite different from those available in the ranks of the traditional structures. Exploration of the new possibilities, for example, required both imagination and a willingness to take risks in uncharted waters, qualities in short supply in management ranks previously devoted to working by rules and procedures and to carefully gauging any risk of commitment. Further, in the front ranks, the personalities and skills of individuals to handle new service roles via the phone, PC, or in person were quite different from those of the traditional bank teller.

The critical resource gap in the banks was not the acquisition of new technology per se, but the human resources to put the technology to work creatively and effectively. The speed with which banks could adapt and innovate was a function of their ability to close this gap. The recognition of this issue, for example, prompted the Midland Bank in the United Kingdom to establish a completely independent business unit called First Bank Direct to exploit the potential in direct banking. This unit was staffed in the first instance by a young development team from within Midland but subsequently by new hires chosen for their aptitudes in the new context. First Bank went on to become a prime example of successful direct banking.

Recycling

Returning to the analytic flow, as your work proceeds you will find yourself in one of three positions. In the first of these the required and available resources will match up in a reasonable way, with the result that you can expect to sail through the next step of gap-closing analysis very quickly. The second outcome is that there are significant but potentially addressable gaps between required and available resources. In the Jantzen case, for example, a proposed transition to a low price strategy might result in cash flow requirements that are beyond the company's immediate capacity. So a key question is whether financing can be found to cover the shortfall. This is what the gap analysis process is all about.

The third outcome of testing the resource-strategy linkage is that you identify resource gaps that you know immediately you cannot close. Say, for example, that your comparison of required research and development strength with current strength suggests that you need to increase the staff by 50 percent. You may know that for financial reasons this is absolutely not feasible. An alternative may be to focus your research spending on fewer projects, but this, in effect, creates a new strategic proposal involving changes in product market focus and logically this proposal needs to be taken through the Diamond-E drill from the beginning. So the result, one way or another in the case of obvious misfits, is to drop the proposal in hand and recycle to the generation of new proposals.

STEP 3: DEVELOP GAP-CLOSING ANALYSIS

As we mentioned above, a well-matched strategy will pass easily through this step and should be carried on to further stages of the Diamond-E drill. The issue for discussion is whether it makes sense for you to stick with a strategy that creates some significant but potentially addressable gaps. The primary matters to consider here are additional costs that you will incur in the attempt to close the gap, the probability that your efforts will be successful and the consequences of going ahead with the strategy but failing to close the gap in a sufficient and timely way.

Additional Costs   In all likelihood the costs of extraordinary efforts to close resource gaps will not have been taken into consideration in formulating the strategic proposal and in preparing performance forecasts. These now need to be factored into your assessment of the strategy. In the case of the Labatt investment in Mexico that we mentioned previously, for example, the cost of a prudent hedging of the currency exposure needs to be subtracted from the returns expected from the investment. If your strategy cannot stand up to these new costs (as probably would have been the case in the Labatt investment) then it should be abandoned and steps taken to generate new proposals.

The Probability of Success   You may recognize a resource gap, you may take extraordinary action to address it, and you may still fail to close the gap and provide the strategy with the support that you were counting on. Consider

Seagram Co.'s high-profile $10-billion acquisition of PolyGram which was aimed at creating a global giant in rock, pop, and classical music. The acquisition price assumed significant operating savings through the merger of PolyGram and Seagram's existing Universal Music group. It was no secret that both companies were short on the required people, disciplines, and procedures to achieve these efficiencies. Seagram took extraordinary steps to close this management gap by bringing in an "army" of consultants.[11] But this had the side effect of upsetting the creative executives who were at the heart of both of the businesses, creating the potential for serious operating problems. There was, in short, a good chance that the efforts to fill the management gaps would fall short in the early going and put the economic justification of the transaction at risk.

A high proportion of gap-closing initiatives will depend on some form of organizational change. The chances of IBP being successful with its consumer products marketing thrust, for example, will depend heavily on its ability to hire and integrate new talent in a hurry. And the chances of Boeing closing its manufacturing productivity gaps and containing its losses to those originally estimated will depend on how fast it can implement some fundamental changes in the way that it operates. Later chapters in this book are intended to help you to analyze and plan organizational changes and to assess the likelihood of success where the closing of resource gaps is an issue.

The Costs of Failure   The failure to close a critical resource gap will handicap a strategy and perhaps cause it to fail outright. The consequences of this need to be identified and weighed in the context of other strategic options and the impact of failure on the company as a whole. You need to ask, "what happens if we can't implement the strategy?"

If the potential consequences of not being able to implement a strategy add up to a "bet-the-company" situation, for example, you obviously need to do a very searching review of the strategy, the implementation issue and of the rationale for assuming the risk. In most cases this review will result in a decision to move on and search for a better way.

In some cases, however, such as when a company is already in crisis, the possibility of drastic downside consequences may be acceptable if the strategy offers a better future than doing nothing! Consider, for example, the circumstances of Canadian Airlines in 1995. The airline was facing accumulating losses and predictable failure if it carried on as it was. Management was considering two strategic options, which they had labelled Plan A and Plan B. Plan A was based on seeking concessions from the company's unions to significantly improve efficiencies, enabling the airline to increase capacity and flight frequencies with minimal increases in cost. The added capacity would then be deployed in an attempt to increase revenues, particularly in the more lucrative business traveller market. There was a serious environmental risk in this strategy, of course, in that Air Canada, Canadian's arch rival, would respond in kind, starting a war of attrition. With this possibility in mind, the internal risks of Plan A were that the concessions and productivity gains might not be achieved and that even if they were, the company wouldn't have the financial capacity to survive a price war. Plan B, on the other hand, called for shrinking the airline to a defensible core through major reductions in people, fleet, and routes. The risks with Plan B were that once a retreat was started competitors would step in and make the situation increasingly untenable and that this process would be accelerated internally by the departure of good people and the evaporation of financial support. Faced with the dilemma of an unacceptable current strategy and two problematic future choices, management moved in the direction of Plan A. In an absolute sense this was a bet-the-company proposition, but in the crisis context it might also be seen as the choice of probable death over certain death.

In less dramatic circumstances the inability to properly implement a strategic proposal may add up to substantial but affordable penalties in cost, market position, reputation, and so on. Here the issue is whether the strategy still makes sense relative to other possibilities. If IBP doesn't pull off its marketing thrust on schedule it will be hurt, but not fatally. Given the overall competitive imperatives driving the strategy, the consequences of stumbling might well be accepted as part of a risk that needs to be taken. At Seagram, the consequences if they botch the PolyGram acquisition and integration might run into the hundreds of millions. While it might be possible for Seagram's to cover such a big amount, the scale of consequences and the likelihood of management miscues surely raise questions about whether there aren't better alternatives available for the investment of $10 billion.

STEP 4: MOVE TO THE NEXT STEP IN THE DIAMOND-E DRILL

You now have a strategy that links well with the environment and with resources. The next step is to check out the strategy-management preferences linkage. But first, let's just recap the benefits of the resource analysis. First, it should have helped you discard any highly inappropriate strategic proposals, saving you the task of taking them further through the Diamond-E drill. Second, you may have created a new strategic proposal or two, based on unique resources that you identified in the course of your analysis. Third, you may have identified certain resources categories that need development and investment— if some of your otherwise good ideas are being rejected for reasons of resource gaps, maybe it's time to work on the missing ingredients.

SUMMARY

Resource analysis is a critical step in the Diamond-E drill. This analysis acts as a filter, culling out inappropriate strategic proposals, and as a generator of new proposals, based on unique resources identified in the course of the analysis. If a proposal makes it through the resource analysis it means that you either already have the resources required to implement it, or that you believe you can develop the required resources in the time available. Successful proposals should now be taken forward for a test of their fit with the preferences of the managers in your business. This process is described in the following chapter.

NOTES

1. P. Selznick, *Leadership in Administration* (New York: Harper & Row, 1957).
2. Igor Ansoff, *Corporate Strategy* (Harmondsworth, U.K.: Penguin, 1965).
3. Leonard Wrigley, "Divisional Autonomy and Diversification," Unpublished Ph.D. dissertation, Harvard Business School, 1970.
4. Gary Hamel and C. K. Prahalad, "The Core Competence of the Corporation," *Harvard Business Review,* vol. 68 (May–June1990), pp. 79–91.
5. David J. Collis and Cynthia Montgomery, "Competing on Resources: Strategy in the 1990s," *Harvard Business Review,* vol. 73 (July–August 1995), pp. 118–128.
6. David S. Jackson, "Apple's New Crop," *Time,* May 18, 1998.
7. Paul Lukas, "The Ghastliest Product Launches," *Fortune,* March 16, 1998.
8. Jonathan Friedland and Louise Lee, "When the Wal-Mart Way Doesn't Play," *Wall Street Journal,* October 8, 1997.
9. For background information see http://www.ibpinc.com.
10. Ronald Henkoff, "Boeing's Big Problem," *Fortune,* January 12, 1998.
11. *Wall Street Journal,* September 26, 1998.

ADDITIONAL READINGS

BLEEKE, JOEL AND DAVID ERNST, *Collaborating to Compete.* New York: John Wiley and Sons, 1993.

COLLIS, DAVID J. AND CYNTHIA A. MONTGOMERY, "Creating Corporate Advantage," *Harvard Business Review,* vol. 76 (May–June 1998), pp. 70–83.

GHEMAWAT, PANKAJ, "Sustainable Advantage," *Harvard Business Review,* vol. 64 (September–October 1986).

STALK JR., GEORGE, "Time: The Next Source of Competitive Advantage," *Harvard Business Review,* vol. 66 (July–August 1988).

STALK JR., GEORGE, PHILIP EVANS AND LAWRENCE SHULMAN, "Competing on Capabilities: The New Rules of Corporate Strategy," *Harvard Business Review,* vol. 70 (March–April 1992), pp. 57–69.

MANAGEMENT PREFERENCE ANALYSIS: THE STRATEGY-MANAGEMENT PREFERENCE LINKAGE

This chapter focuses on the third major relationship in the Diamond-E framework: the link between management preferences and strategic proposals. We will outline how to ensure that the skills and the energy of management are matched with attractive strategies for their businesses. As a matter of perspective, we will assume that your personal preferences are consistent with the strategic proposals under consideration and that these proposals are also consistent with external and resource considerations. This leaves two significant potential conflicts for you to address.

Inconsistency Between Proposed and Preferred Strategy

The first type of conflict is that which occurs when a strategic proposal is inconsistent with the preferences of one or more of the influential managers in your business. We described this situation in our discussion of the Diamond-E drill in Chapter 3.

Every strategic proposal implies a set of strategic preferences, which may or may not conform with the preferences of managers in the firm. These conflicts need to be identified and corrected or the pursuit of the strategy could be hamstrung by management indifference or outright opposition.

Sometimes you can resolve these conflicts by modifying the strategic proposal, but this tactic is limited by the need for the proposal to remain consistent with the other elements of the Diamond-E. More often than not you will need to work with the managers involved to bring their preferences into line with the strategic requirements. Persuasion and training may suffice for relatively simple problems, but more significant system and structural changes will be needed in more difficult situations. As a last resort, you may have to replace the managers.

As the severity of the actions escalate so, too, do the demands on you and on the underlying organizational capabilities in the business. These requirements need to be checked out as part of a subsequent organization analysis before the matter can be closed and a final decision made on the strategic proposal under study.

Inconsistency Between Preferred Strategy and Other Realities

Another and more complex conflict occurs when management preferences are actually consistent with a strategic proposal, but the proposal itself is inconsistent with external forces or business capabilities. There are two quite different manifestations of this problem. In the first, some managers become committed to a new strategic proposal that is otherwise inconsistent with business conditions. In the second, some managers want to persevere with a strategy that is becoming obsolete in the face of changing conditions. In these cases the preference-strategy linkage is strong, but the strategy won't work. Any suggestions for change come into conflict with the preferences and momentum of some influential people. This takes you back to the beginning and puts you into the situation of dealing with preferences that conflict with otherwise sensible strategic ideas.

A serious difficulty arises when you (or other "objective" analysts) identify either of the conflicts noted above, but find yourself in a weak position to influence the other managers. The result, all too often, is another opportunity lost, or of a business driven into crisis because management preferences were frozen on inappropriate strategies.

The first part of this chapter discusses the role and the roots of strategic preferences. We then elaborate on the analytic and action steps required to focus, first, on conflicts associated with individual managers, and then on the difficulties created by different preferences within a single management group. Finally, we discuss the utility of the concept of management preferences in analyzing competitive behaviour.

THE ROLE OF MANAGEMENT PREFERENCES

You and your management colleagues drive strategy. Your analytic work shapes the strategic direction of your businesses and your actions put it into place. In this, your personal preferences—what you want the business to accomplish and how you think this should be done—play an inevitable and critical role. To suggest that managers should operate (or do operate) according to some impersonal dictate is a convenient simplification in some of the more abstract work on business strategy, but it flies in the face of reality. This reality, as Andrews puts it, is that "there is no way to divorce the decision determining the most sensible economic strategy for a company from the personal values of those who make the choice."[1]

Consider the role of management preferences as they have influenced the fortunes of Magna International Inc., the $8 billion auto parts manufacturer. Magna's founder, Frank Stronach, was a classic entrepreneur with a strong appetite for growth, a willingness to take risks, and an unshakable confidence in his demonstrably impressive business skills. Stronach had built Magna into a strong and growing auto parts supplier by the mid 1980s when his eye started to wander. He took Magna into restaurant, publishing, and real estate ventures, went heavily into debt to fund the core business, and entered politics as a candidate for member of parliament. When an industry downturn struck in 1990, Magna was hit hard and its shares fell from over $20 to $2. While Stronach disagrees with criticisms that the side ventures were of any significance,[2] Magna quickly reverted to its base business. Magna rebounded and grew rapidly in the 1990s, focusing on auto parts and exploiting a clever combination of internal development and acquisitions. By the fall of 1997, Magna's shares were trading at over $100. Shortly afterward, they fell $20 on news that Stronach was planning to take the company into eight non-automotive ventures including an $800 million theme park near Vienna, an executive airline, and real estate development.[3] Investors were only partly reassured when Stronach wrote a special letter to shareholders vowing that the focus of the company would be on auto parts (and in this respect his personal vision for the company was to more than triple to $30 billion in revenues), and further, that unrelated ventures would be held separate in a venture capital division.[4] The question was, would Stronach stay (or could the board keep Stronach) inside the envelope of tolerable, if aggressive, risk?

Management preferences clearly cut two ways. On the positive side, preferences serve to focus and motivate the efforts of the firm. The realities of the external environment and of internal circumstances seldom determine a single feasible course of action. Rather, they present a set of opportunities and constraints from which can develop a variety of feasible strategic options. Within these boundaries there is a need for a driving force to take hold of the situation and press for choices and performance.

On the negative side, management preferences may lead to pressures for inappropriate ventures, potential inflexibility, a focus on personal versus shareholder interests, and so on. In extreme cases, these circumstances may put you and your business at risk.

THE ROOTS OF STRATEGIC PREFERENCE

Strategic preferences have their roots in the personal attributes of managers and in their job contexts. Personal attributes generate tendencies towards certain types of action; the job context adds a web of behavioural incentives and constraints. Together, these characteristics influence how managers perceive business situations, explore strategic possibilities, and evaluate options. The result for any specific manager is a set of strategic preferences regarding the nature and aggressiveness of the goals for the business, the product markets in which it should operate, the value proposition it should put forward, and the core activities of its operations. In the following paragraphs we will discuss how the basic needs, beliefs, and job contexts of managers shape their strategic preferences.

Basic Needs

Basic needs refer to central aspects of a manager's personality. They include the need for achievement, power, security, and recognition. These needs operate as fundamental influences on strategic preferences. Managers with a strong need for achievement or power will likely favour expansionary programs and accept the risks they may imply. Managers with a strong need for security and order will favour more cautious and methodical strategic development.

A manager's basic needs are fairly stable and enduring, and support a consistent approach to strategic decisions. This consistency can be valuable, but it can also pose problems if managers persist in the face of conflict between their preferences and other strategic determinants. It is not likely that basic needs can be materially changed. Your only practical options in these circumstances may be changing the nature of the job or changing the manager on the job.

Prescriptions like this may sound more severe than they are. Moving managers to improve the match between personal needs and strategic requirements may be practical for both the managers and the business. There is little point in shouldering aggressive and risk-oriented managers with the task of maintaining a mature, stable business, or asking careful and methodical managers to lead a risky project. As Harry Levinson points out: "It's like trying to put your best guard into a quarterback's slot—it just can't work."[5]

Beliefs

Over the years, managers build up beliefs about their own competences, about the capabilities of their colleagues, and about the right way to handle strategic issues. These beliefs are not independent of personality; neither are they direct extensions of it. Accordingly, the degree to which managers are attached to their beliefs may vary from deep and emotional conviction to rather casual endorsement, and the degree to which you can influence and change their beliefs will range from relative ease to extreme difficulty, a factor which can be important when we come to questions of modifying strategic preferences.

Beliefs direct management preferences towards particular strategic initiatives and responses. The strategic direction given to a firm will be heavily influenced by the fields in which top management feels competent and comfortable. Consider, for example, the claim of Hayes and Abernathy that the wheeling and dealing in acquisitions and mergers that preoccupy top managers in some companies can be related to their legal and financial backgrounds. They are doing what they think is important and what they feel competent to do, often at the expense, the authors contend, of the more fundamental development of their companies.[6]

Table 6.1 demonstrates how some common managerial beliefs fit into our strategy format. It is pretty clear that beliefs like these, held by powerful managers, would significantly influence the development of strategy.

Job Context

Job assignments define the scope and nature of a manager's responsibilities, the manner in which performance will be measured and assessed, and the principles on which rewards are allocated. Further, each job is set within a context of formal and informal relationships, and of expectations from bosses, peers, and subordinates. All of these factors may influence strategic preferences. As well, the pressures of the job context may help explain a condition we call *frozen preference,* in which a manager, having openly endorsed a strategic option, will find it difficult or virtually impossible to change.

TABLE 6.1
Examples of Top Management Beliefs Regarding Strategy

Goals

We must grow in volume and ROI.
We must maintain a conservative financial structure.
We must be measured against the best.
Stable employment is a basic employee right.

Product Market Focus

Don't diversify except where our technology can be applied.
We must not be dependent on one single product line.
We can't run a lot of businesses we don't know anything about.
We can manage in a range of industries.

Value Proposition

Market share comes through technically superior products.
It is important to have a known brand name.
Quality of our product is our number one concern.
We must compete on innovation in processes and basic products, not price.

Core Activities

We must be a leader in manufacturing to keep costs down and quality up.
We need to control every input to our product.
Our abilities in marketing will make the difference in the future.
We are prepared to pay a price to remain flexible.

Format based on Gordon Donaldson and Jay W. Lorsch, *Decision Making at the Top* (New York, 1983). Copyright © 1983 by Basic Books, Inc., Publishers.

Job Definition   The status and responsibilities of their jobs affect the way managers look at strategic issues. In the Magna case just cited, for example, Frank Stronach was clearly in favour of moving the company into very significant non-automotive ventures. He planned to put his European finance director, Robert Gruber, in charge of the projects. But Gruber disagreed with the non-automotive thrust and with the supposed potential of the new projects. He resigned rather than take on the responsibility for them.[7] These were clear-cut differences of opinion, generated in part by the different needs and beliefs of the two managers, and in part by the job perspectives from which they viewed the situation.

Most strategic proposals will have different consequences for managers in different job positions. Strategic changes usually create winners and losers. For example, a shift from an emphasis on differentiation to a reliance on low relative price will change the budgets and status of several functional positions. It is only reasonable, then, for you to expect that job-related filters and biases will be imposed on strategic assessments. It is simple realities like this that help to explain why firms tend to like growth strategies and dislike retrenchment—the former offer the best prospects of making the most managers into winners.

The manner in which job responsibilities are specified and performance is measured and rewarded will also influence strategic preferences. A manager who is charged with producing maximum short-term profit from a business, and whose performance is measured and rewarded accordingly, will understandably emphasize short-term tactics. Alternatively, a manager with a compensation package that depends on growth can be expected to press for volume building and investment initiatives. It follows that the design and specification of job responsibilities, measures, and rewards is a major tool that you can use for shaping and changing strategic preferences.

Job Relations   The expectations of bosses, peers, and subordinates may be less visible than formal job characteristics, but they are no less forceful. The expectations conveyed in subtle and not-so-subtle ways from board to chief executive, from chief executive to president, and from president to general or functional managers will have a significant effect on a manager's approach to strategic questions. A particular attitude to risk might be conveyed in a business, for example, that cues a manager to the kind of projects that will likely be given support and those that might be rejected out of hand.

Most managers need the cooperation and support of their colleagues to execute their programs. But they also compete with these same colleagues for status, resources, and jobs. As a consequence, managers tend to assess strategic initiatives with an eye to their impact on the balance of relationships and status among their peers.

The reliance of managers on their subordinates can also influence their strategic preferences. Subordinates have expectations of what their boss should provide:

security, opportunity, and an interesting job, for example. To ensure employee co-operation, you have to respond in some degree to these expectations and include them among the now complex balances that influence strategic direction.

Frozen Preference

For an organization to function effectively, superiors, peers, and subordinates alike must be able to count on a manager's reliability and determination. If a manager changes positions after taking an open and firm stance on a strategic issue, except in the case of quite overwhelming evidence, he or she may be seen as poorly prepared, weak, or lacking sufficient power and influence to prevail. Any of these factors will damage a manager's credibility.

As management preferences are expressed in budgets, personnel changes, and investments, the firm's commitment to a position increases and it becomes more and more difficult to change direction. Fresh analysis or evidence may indicate that the position is questionable, and that it should be abandoned, with accumulated expenditures simply regarded as "sunk cost." This, however, is not how accountants will report the situation, nor necessarily how the various parties to it will react. There may be strong pressures to continue and these pressures will feed on the normally ambiguous circumstances that a manager faces. Managers may find themselves facing a dilemma in which a change of position that makes sense in the abstract could result in substantial personal loss.

Watch for instances of creeping commitment and for circumstances in which frozen preferences are distorting strategic choices. If you can address the problems before people have made a large and visible investment in a position, you may be able to change the direction without great disruption. Otherwise, you may be forced to make changes through radical alteration of the job context or the reassignment of the managers involved.

Implications

Management preferences are formed by the interaction of needs, beliefs, and situational pressures. These preferences have meaningful implications for strategic choice, whether they operate for the betterment of the organization or to its detriment. They should not be treated as unchanging or unchangeable. If the core influences change (if, for example, experience brings about a change in the beliefs of a manager) or are changed (for instance, if a manager's compensation package is altered), then preferences can be expected to change as well.

Managers' preferences are specific to their individual personalities, experiences, and situations. Differences in these factors among managers will lead to differences in their strategic preferences, which adds an extra dimension to your analysis. You must identify differences in preferences among the key managers, assess the implications of the differences, and, where necessary, find grounds for their reconciliation.

MATCHING PREFERENCES AND STRATEGY

A particularly challenging aspect of management preference analysis is that the task often calls for managers to reflect on their *own* values and attitudes. As Guth and Tagiuri note: "Few of us make the effort of studying our own values to the point of being able to be explicit and articulate about them. The busy executive is no exception . . . . Many top-level managers do not have an explicit and useful way of thinking about personal values and about the influences these have on the strategic choice processes of the company. As a result, this important element is often left unexamined."[8]

In spite of the difficulties of candid introspection, good managers appreciate that personal preferences enter into strategic decisions. They try to capture the benefits of serving these preferences while avoiding distortions that may be created by them. They also appreciate that no amount of introspection, analysis, and advice will help managers who refuse to be flexible and who insist on imposing their fixed preferences on a situation.

For the moment we will deal with the consistency of the preferences of an individual manager with other strategic determinants. We will work through the analytic steps presented in Figure 6.1 from your perspective and from that of an ex-

FIGURE 6.1

Management Preference Analysis

Step 1: Identify the Required Management Preferences
Work from the strategic proposal to develop a list of required management preferences. This can usually be organized in terms of the preferences implied by each of the four elements of strategy.

GENERATE NEW STRATEGIC PROPOSAL(S)

Step 2: Test the Strategy-Preferences Linkage
Compare the required preferences with the observed preferences of influential managers and management groups. Identify current and anticipated gaps between the two. For serious misfits recycle to develop a more attractive proposal.

Step 3: Develop Gap-Closing Analysis
Assess the feasibility of closing any material gaps. If the costs, chances of success, and consequences of failure are acceptable, carry the proposal forward. If not, recycle to generate new proposals.

Step 4: Move to Next Step in Diamond-E Drill
Assess the strategy-organization linkage.

98

ternal advisor. Later, we will discuss the complications created when there are different strategic preferences among the group of managers running a given business.

As in Chapter 5, there are two subsidiary formats that you will find helpful in working through the analytic process. The first format, presented in Table 6.2, focuses on the use of the proposed strategy to identify and describe the relevant management preferences. The second format, which is intended for concurrent use and ultimately as a summary document, is illustrated in Table 6.3. It emphasizes the links between preferences and specific managers or management groups.

STEP 1: IDENTIFY THE REQUIRED MANAGEMENT PREFERENCES

The logical flow for identifying the management preferences that count is from the proposed strategy to the required preferences. Work from your understanding of each element of the proposed strategy, as illustrated in Table 6.2. As you do this, try to focus your analysis or your list will rapidly become cluttered and unworkable.

TABLE 6.2
Management Preference Analysis by Strategy Component

Strategic Proposal	Required Preferences	Observed Preferences	Major Gaps	Gap-Closing Analysis
Goals	What are the most critical goal preferences (e.g., for growth, risk, market dominance) required by strategic proposal under consideration; what are the gaps between these requirements and observed preferences; and what are the risks and consequences of not being able to close these gaps in a timely way?			
Product/Market Focus	What are the most critical product/market preferences (e.g., for a specific market focus, diversification) required by the strategic proposal under consideration; what are the gaps between these requirements and observed preferences; and what are the risks and consequences of not being able to close these gaps in a timely way?			
Value Proposition	What are the most critical value proposition preferences (e.g., for price, features, execution) required by the strategic proposal under consideration; what are the gaps between these preferences and observed preferences; and what are the risks and consequences of not being able to close these gaps in a timely way?			
Core Activities	What are the most critical core activities preferences (e.g., for activities to internalize, degree of integration) required by the strategic proposal under consideration; what are the gaps between these requirements and observed preferences; and what are the risks and consequences of not being able to close these gaps in a timely way?			

Concentrate on the strategic features that you know are (1) new and different, and (2) most likely to be controversial. Strategic proposals that are essentially extensions or variants on the current strategy are unlikely to generate serious conflicts with existing management preferences. The strategic preferences required for the strategic proposal are pretty much the strategic preferences in place. But if your strategy calls for new ways of thinking and behaving in the management team and/or changes of management status and power, it is likely to run into some very definite preference issues. The new and contentious elements have to be carefully mapped into new required preferences. Clearly, the greater the skill with which you can pin down the sensitive areas of strategy and preference, the faster you will get to the preference gaps that really matter.

A second approach for isolating important preference dimensions is to work from your knowledge of the managers and management groups that will be importantly involved in the implementation of the strategy. Start by listing these individuals or groups as suggested by the Table 6.3 format. Then you can work from the demands of the strategy as it affects these particular managers and your knowledge of the managers to isolate the elements of management preference that are going to be of greatest importance. To some degree this overlaps the gap analysis to follow, but that is all right since we are not trying to draw lines between the suggested phases of analysis.

STEP 2: TEST THE STRATEGY-PREFERENCES LINKAGE

Your aim in this step of preference analysis is to identify the important gaps between the required and observed preferences. If your Step 1 work has been ef-

TABLE 6.3
Management Preference Analysis by Manager

Management Subject	Required Preferences	Observed Preferences	Major Gaps	Gap-Closing Analysis
Manager 1				
Manager 2				
Etc.				
Group 1				
Group 2				
Etc.				

fective this will be a relatively straightforward task. Let's return, for example, to the case of Jantzen Technologies, which we introduced in Chapter 4.

Harry Jantzen, the company founder, has built a successful business by focusing on a narrow product range and pursuing continuous product innovation through close technical relationships with selected customers. The company has grown to the point where it has a global production base, but future growth and profitability are threatened by a maturing technical and market environment. Nothing is ever for sure, but the Jantzen situation seems clearly to call for major strategic changes. In particular, Jantzen must consider (1) broadening its market, in terms of the number and type of customers, and broadening its contacts within these customer organizations to encompass purchasing and manufacturing personnel; (2) improving its capacity to compete on price through design, purchasing, and manufacturing development and rationalization; and (3) reducing its insistence on total integration to take advantage of technical and cost innovation among sub-component manufacturers and distributors.

There are some far-reaching implications in these strategic proposals for the leadership role of Harry Jantzen. He must be, and be seen to be, enthusiastic about a new and very commercial approach to the market and to operations, under which customers are selected, products are designed, and manufacturing is driven on the basis of market and profit potential. These requirements are at odds with Harry Jantzen's experience and with his beliefs about how to run a business. He would much prefer the technology-driven success formula of the past. The obvious, but vital, question for the business is whether Jantzen is now prepared to change his thinking and to significantly reorient his efforts and those of the business.

As the areas of congruence and conflict between required and observed preferences are identified, you can start to consider the action that will be necessary to deal with the situation. In the case of gaps that you think will be irreconcilable, there is no option but to recycle and start to work on new proposals. This will not be a happy decision and will certainly be a last resort since the proposal that you have in hand looks attractive from the point of view of your environmental and resource analysis. In the more likely circumstance of significant but potentially workable preference gaps you need to carry on to consider the feasibility of steps to bring about consistency.

STEP 3: DEVELOP GAP-CLOSING ANALYSIS

In this section we will deal first with the relatively straightforward, but by no means simple, process of gap-closing analysis with respect to an individual manager. Then we will proceed to the more complex issues involving groups of managers.

Framing the Gap-Closing Issues—Individual Managers

In the presentation below we have classified potential conflicts by order of severity and discuss the diagnostic implications that arise from them.

Minimal Conflict   This is a fortunate situation in which there appear to be only minor discrepancies between required and observed preferences of the manager in question. Even so, these differences should be carefully considered. One tool that you might use in this respect is to forecast the firm's performance assuming that the observed differences persist. Will the performance of the business under the strategic proposal be affected by the conflicts observed? This is the ultimate test of how seriously the conflicts should be taken and the lengths to which you should go in addressing them.

Moderate Conflict   In this situation there are significant conflicts between required and observed preferences, but it seems, at least on first analysis, that they can be reconciled with something short of radical action. When you run into such conflicts it is useful to stand back and reassess the situation. Can you influence the manager's preferences to reduce the conflict to workable levels? Is it possible, for example, to modify the manager's preferences by exposure to the facts, reasoning, advocacy, or simple changes in job context? Or are there nuances in the strategy itself that can be reworked to make it more acceptable, yet still consistent with your earlier environmental and resource considerations? Try working closely with the manager involved to craft a sensible compromise solution to the original conflicts. If this approach does not succeed, you will have to deal with the problem as a serious conflict that calls for more aggressive action.

Serious Conflict   A serious conflict exists when it is impossible to find a moderate and workable accommodation of preferences and strategy. Persuasion, reason, better information, and modest changes in job context haven't worked. One possible remedy in such a situation is to completely rethink and change the strategic proposal. However, the new proposal will have to be compatible with environment and resource considerations, and, not incidentally, the preferences of other influential managers. Other remedies lie in making major organizational changes, up to and including the reassignment of the manager involved.

These circumstances confront you with a pretty difficult situation. The manager in question may choose to fight the strategic proposal, particularly if he or she is in a position of power, on the grounds that the proposal is bad for the company. Strategic situations are often ambiguous enough that strong individuals may be able to colour the circumstances with their own biases. It is not too hard to imagine Harry Jantzen, for example, fighting the evidence of a changing market and arguing for an interpretation of the environmental conditions that supports the strategic responses that he would *like.*

Another option for the manager experiencing such conflicts is to go along with the strategy and live with the discrepancy between it and his or her own convictions. Of course, that manager will probably not perform well over time with such suppressed inconsistencies. Your best options will probably boil down to organizational changes including the reassignment of the objecting manager. This move, while possibly painful in the short run, is probably best, both for the individual involved and for business performance.

The whole situation becomes much more problematic, however, if you report to or are otherwise dependent on the problem manager. Being forthright may be desirable, but it may also mean the end of your career! Remaining silent about the conflicts that you have identified or, worse, rationalizing your perception of the realities to fit the preferences might offer short-term relief, but will undoubtedly be counterproductive in the long run. In these situations, senior managers get the kind of advice they deserve. If their leadership style and management systems support candour, it will be relatively easy for you as a subordinate to discharge at least your minimum responsibility—which is to make it clear that the manager's strategic preferences are out of line with the strategic realities. If managers are repressive, it is unlikely that you will tell them the whole truth, unless you are a truly independent person, and even then it is unlikely that the message will be heard.

Gap-Closing Actions and Risks—Individual Managers

Many of the actions that you will want to take to resolve the conflicts of required and observed management preferences will involve organizational change. From the broad perspective of organization theory the underlying problem is one of aligning business goals (strategy) and individual goals (preferences). Discrepancies between required and observed preferences affect the organizational capabilities of the business—the collective ability of the people involved to carry out the required tasks. When you move on to organization analysis, the next stage of the drill, you will need to ask whether the required capabilities exist or can be developed in the time available. For now you need to set up that analysis by pinning down the capabilities that will be required to implement the actions. And, given experience with the drill and organization change from prior strategic analyses, you need to reject and recycle proposals that don't deserve further analysis because they are simply too risky to proceed with.

In the case of Harry Jantzen, the first step would be to provide him with a convincing picture of what is happening in his component system market and what the consequences will be for growth and profitability. You have some data

103

and some serious concerns based on a very broadly based size-up of the situation, but it is unlikely that arguments at this level of abstraction will sway Harry Jantzen; you need tight and unequivocal evidence. This calls for an organizational capability to acquire and process the required information, which might look simple at first glance, but actually will be quite difficult to do. Why? Because the Jantzen organization has never really done this before—they have only looked at very narrow slices of information such as that gathered by their technical salesmen talking to their customers' engineering groups.

Suppose, further, that that the new information strongly supports the case for change, but Harry Jantzen remains unconvinced. His preferences are frozen on the traditional formula for success and in various ways he indicates that he is not prepared to change his views. Now the conflict escalates to critical proportions. Should Jantzen step aside? If so, does the organizational capability exist to carry out such a difficult task? At a minimum, the board must believe that this is a necessary step and there must be a successor ready to move in and make the desired changes. (In reality such a step was not necessary.) Whether this capability is present or can be developed is, again, a question for subsequent organization analysis.

As you settle the list of the organizational capabilities required to address the fit of preferences and strategy, the analysis can move on to the subject of Chapter 7—do you have, or can you develop, the capabilities required to proceed with the strategy? Before we take this step, however, it is useful to review the common and complex challenges of bringing the preferences of a diverse group of managers into line with one strategy.

Framing the Gap-Closing Issues—Groups of Managers

You shouldn't be surprised to find differences among the strategic preferences of the various managers of a firm. Each of these managers, after all, will be working from a somewhat different personal background and job context. As a matter of fact, you should *expect* that marketing and operations managers, for example, will read the facts of a situation differently, see different options for action, and weigh consequences unevenly. This is one of the prime arguments for articulating a strategy in the first place—to provide a unifying theme that will help to bring these different strategic preferences together, and establish a common basis for management action. But a good strategic process alone may not be enough to achieve and sustain a workable consistency of preference in a diverse management group.

It follows that you should identify the strategic preferences of the key management groups in a business and determine how consistent these preferences are with those required by the strategic proposal under consideration. This is anticipated in Table 6.3 which calls for analysis by management group. Again, the art of the analysis is to be carefully selective in choosing which particular groups and preference issues to study.

You will probably encounter some obstacles in the process of identifying the real preferences of diverse groups of managers. Some will be in subordinate and perhaps vulnerable positions and reluctant to openly express their views. In firms that have learned how to support an open expression of opinions and to avoid the difficulties of frozen preferences, this obstacle will not be a serious problem. Preferences may be carefully and even ambiguously posed, but they will be genuine. In relatively unhealthy firms, you may find that managers and groups operate more or less continuously with hidden agendas. Even senior and experienced people may be less than candid. In unhealthy businesses it is often difficult to tell what a manager's real position and preferences are, even when he or she openly supports a strategic initiative. The great fear is that that manager will nod *yes,* and then walk away and do nothing to help implement the strategy.

In our discussion we will assume that you are dealing with a management system that is healthy enough for the essential preferences of the managers to be identified, even if this takes careful diagnostic work. If a firm is so politicized that it is impossible to develop a reasonably valid impression of management preferences, the problem is so fundamental that it raises the question of the viability of the business, which is beyond our immediate scope.

The following paragraphs discuss the conflicts that might arise from differences within a management group in three increasingly difficult categories.

Minimal Conflict   This is a welcome situation that emerges when there are minimal differences among the strategic preferences of the key managers and groups in a business. Such a commonality of preference is an important feature of companies that have had strong leaders for some time, or that have otherwise built up clear traditions and culture. In these companies, the managers that succeed over time are those who conform to the dominant ethos.

Homogeneity across a management group can be a mixed blessing, however. It can be a powerful asset *if* the preferences line up with the strategic proposal under consideration. Minor conflicts can probably be ironed out easily, because the group is used to the give-and-take of working together. However, if these preferences are inconsistent with strategic needs, you now face the problems of what Irving Janis calls "groupthink," in which the concurrence of a cohesive group overrides a realistic appraisal of new realities.[9]

Moderate Conflict   At this level it is often possible to bring diverse preferences into line with strategy by further documentation, persuasion, changes in the stakes for particular individuals, or changes in management assignments. A very important reason for having a strategic planning process in a business (and for having the process driven by line managers) is to work out preference conflicts as they happen. Even if a conflict still exists at the end of the process, the managers with problems will fully understand why the proposed course is deemed necessary, and may be more flexible in adapting to it.

It is difficult to resolve conflicts between strategic requirements and the preferences of a group of managers by modifying strategy; the most likely route to reconciliation is through organizational action. From a diagnostic standpoint this means, first, identifying the actions that are likely to bring preferences into alignment and second, identifying the organizational capabilities that will be required for implementation of the action. Consider the task of bringing together differences of preference across business functions.

It is commonplace for R&D, operations, and marketing managers to take a different view of strategic problems and of proposed solutions. Depending on the depth of the differences and the flexibility of the people involved, reaching a reasonable consensus may require, for example, providing better information about the market, changing incentives to emphasize joint performance, or, at the opposite extreme, restructuring to manage with smaller and more identifiably responsible leaders and teams. Each step of action across this spectrum puts increasing demands on the organization's ability to deliver and takes you further into the issue of whether those capabilities are in place or whether they can be developed.

There is also a catch in the process of using organizational action to address preference discrepancies. The organization that is in place in a business is in many ways the creation of the managers you are dealing with and it reflects their preferences for how the business should be run. The implementation of a new direction involves a capability on the part of the people in the organization to address and change those organizational preferences as well as the targeted strategic preferences. This is no small task. We shall return to it in our discussion of strategic change in later chapters.

Serious Conflict If managers are at such great odds with each other that there is no reasonable strategy that they can commonly endorse, you may be watching the total disintegration of an organization. The causes for the difficulties probably go far beyond the individual preferences of one manager or another. The management team may have tried in the past to paper over their differences, but the conflicts have kept reemerging. The situation calls for a comprehensive review of the whole business and for action, as necessary, across an equally broad front.

MANAGEMENT PREFERENCES AND COMPETITIVE ANALYSIS

A corollary of the principle that strategy must relate to management preferences is that a competitor's strategy will also reflect its management's preferences. Analyzing the character, habits, ways of thinking, and stakes of a competitor's management team can help to predict the strategy that a competitor will employ and the conviction with which it will be pursued. (In World War II, the German field marshal Erwin Rommel was renowned for his mastery of tank warfare. He wrote a book on the subject. Few who have seen the movie *Patton* will forget George C. Scott, playing Patton, gloating after outwitting Rommel in a battle in North Africa: "Rommel, you magnificent bastard, I read your book!")

It is clearly important to understand the predispositions of the key managers in competitive firms. To this end it is useful to record and study their strategic initiatives and responses in prior circumstances. Most managers have a limited strategic repertoire, particularly when they have been rewarded for what they have done before. In 1994 Wal-Mart entered the Canadian market. Its strategy was highly predictable—to repeat the formula employed so successfully in the United States. It was up to the incumbent Canadian retailers to decide how to respond. Most tried to out–Wal-Mart Wal-Mart. In short order the Woolco discount chain was out of business (sold to Wal-Mart) and so was the K mart chain (bought by Zellers). The largest remaining competitor, Zellers, fought on under its slogan, "Because . . . the lowest price is the law." But Zellers sales and profits continued to suffer and in 1998 it capitulated, dropping the slogan and announcing that henceforth it would "out-flank" Wal-Mart and compete with an emphasis on fashion and style.[10] What the incumbent retailers seemed to have missed in all of this was the focus, conviction, and force with which Wal-Mart would proceed—which was just as evident as its visible strategy if you studied its U.S. management.

It is often possible to anticipate how a competitive manager is inclined to act on the basis of past personal history. This analysis should be coupled with what can be deduced about his or her personal stakes in the current situation. Is the manager on a fast track, looking for quick results? Is she or he near retirement? Are any unusual pressures being exerted by board members, shareholders, or bankers? Long-standing competitors use this understanding to predict strategy down to the finest nuances. And by tracking new management appointments, such as when a competitor hires a new marketing vice president with a reputation for building market share by cutting prices, you can develop a pretty good idea about what is going to happen next.

A competitor's activities in a specific product market will depend on the number and nature of the issues with which its management is contending, and on the priority it gives to the specific market in question. If it often useful to analyze the relationships among functional and/or product groups in a competitive firm and to predict the response of this system to emerging threats. To the degree that competitors are harnessed by frozen preferences, their actions are predictable, and advantages can be gained by avoiding their areas of priority. The big hope of many of the new Internet-based businesses, for example, from automobiles to books to banks and on and on, is that that they can get a head start and build a defensible position before the conventional competitors in their industries notice and react with force.

SUMMARY

The object of management preference analysis is to identify conflicts between the motivations of key managers and the strategies that are important to their businesses, and to point to the actions that are required to resolve them. Conflicts arise when managers oppose a strategic proposal that is otherwise very desirable for the business, or when they freeze on strategies that are inconsistent with business opportunities and constraints.

The resolution of these conflicts calls for a careful analysis of the roots and changeability of the preferences involved and for action that is tailored to this understanding. It is sometimes possible to find strategic modifications that will accommodate existing preferences, but more often it is necessary to take organizational action to achieve consistency. Such action might range from persuasion to changes in job context to reassignment.

The final stage of analysis is to assess the feasibility of achieving consistency between preferences and strategy. In some cases the costs will be too high or the chances of success too low and you will have to recycle to generate new strategic proposals. On closer calls you will have to make judgments about the capacity of the business to develop new organizational capabilities, and this takes us into the subject matter of the next chapter.

NOTES

1. Kenneth R. Andrews, *The Concept of Corporate Strategy*, rev. ed. (Homewood, Illinois: Richard D. Irwin, Inc., 1980), p. 74.

2. *Globe and Mail,* January 23, 1998.

3. *Globe and Mail,* April 8, 1998.

4. *Globe and Mail,* March 12, 1998.

5. "Wanted: A Manager to Fit Each Strategy," *Business Week,* February 25, 1980, pp.166–173.

6. Robert H. Hayes and William J. Abernathy, "Managing Our Way to Economic Decline," *Harvard Business Review,* vol. 58 (July–August 1980), pp. 67–77.

7. *Globe and Mail,* January 27, 1998.

8. William D. Guth and Renato Tagiuri, "Personal Values and Corporate Strategy," *Harvard Business Review* (September–October 1965).

9. Irving L. Janis, "Groupthink," *Psychology Today* (November 1971), pp. 43–46, 74–76.

10. *Globe and Mail,* May 20, 1998.

ADDITIONAL READINGS

ANDREWS, KENNETH R., *The Concept of Corporate Strategy,* rev. ed. Homewood, Illinois: Richard D. Irwin, Inc., 1980, Chapter 4.

DONALDSON, GORDON AND JAY W. LORSCH, *Decision Making at the Top: The Shaping of Strategic Direction.* New York: Basic Books Inc., 1983, Chapters 5 and 8.

KANTROW, ALAN M., *The Constraints of Corporate Tradition.* New York: Harper & Row Publishers Inc., 1984.

STRATEGY AND ORGANIZATION

By this point you have developed one or more strategic proposals that look good. They make sense given what is happening in your firm's external environment, and while you would probably have some resource and preference gaps to fill to implement any of the proposals, none of the challenges you see are overwhelming. Now you need to determine what organizational changes, if any, would be required to implement each proposal, and if such changes are feasible in the time you have available.

Our focus in this chapter is on what we call organizational capabilities. By this we mean what your people are collectively capable of when they work together. Being quick at something, like developing a new product and getting it to market, is an organizational capability. So is the ability to innovate. In the language of the Diamond-E model, the people in your organization are resources, but what they are capable of doing together is an organizational capability. A decision to hire five automotive design engineers, for example, is a resource decision. What they are actually capable of, once they are working for you, is the addition they make to your capabilities. One firm may get a lot more from five new engineers than another.

As shown in Figure 7.1, we will address four sets of questions in this chapter: (1) what organizational capabilities would you need in order to implement the strategic proposal that you are considering? (2) what are the gaps between these needed organizational capabilities and the capabilities that you currently have? (3) what changes would you need to make in organization structure, management processes, and leadership behaviour to develop the organizational capabilities that you would need to fill these gaps? and (4) would these changes in fact lead to the development of the new capabilities in the time available?

Before turning to these questions, however, we will discuss further the notion of organizational capabilities, and the relationship between these capabilities, the culture of your organization, and the behaviour of your employees. These relationships are by no means simple, and the judgments that you are ultimately going to make about the ability of your firm to develop new capabilities based on new behaviour and a changed culture are as difficult as any discussed in this book.

ORGANIZATIONAL CAPABILITIES

New strategies usually require that new things be done well. You have already thought about the new resources that would be needed to support your strategic proposal, and the new preferences that would be required of senior management. But filling gaps in those two areas may not be enough. Your new resources, put into the hands of people who still act in the "same old way," may not be of much use. You might build a new factory, for example, but if the people in it do not understand that customer responsiveness is the key to your new value proposition, your strategy will never be properly implemented.

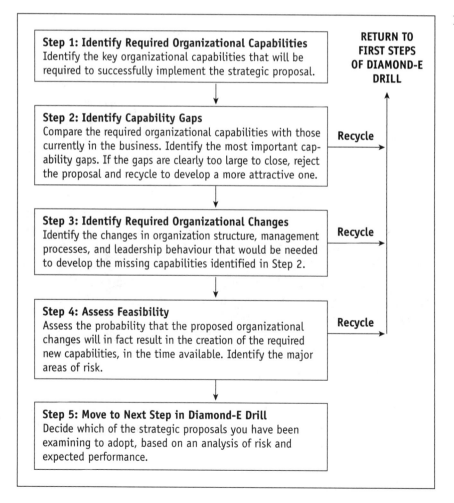

FIGURE 7.1

Strategy-Organization Analysis

Step 1: Identify Required Organizational Capabilities
Identify the key organizational capabilities that will be required to successfully implement the strategic proposal.

RETURN TO FIRST STEPS OF DIAMOND-E DRILL

Step 2: Identify Capability Gaps
Compare the required organizational capabilities with those currently in the business. Identify the most important capability gaps. If the gaps are clearly too large to close, reject the proposal and recycle to develop a more attractive one.

Recycle

Step 3: Identify Required Organizational Changes
Identify the changes in organization structure, management processes, and leadership behaviour that would be needed to develop the missing capabilities identified in Step 2.

Recycle

Step 4: Assess Feasibility
Assess the probability that the proposed organizational changes will in fact result in the creation of the required new capabilities, in the time available. Identify the major areas of risk.

Recycle

Step 5: Move to Next Step in Diamond-E Drill
Decide which of the strategic proposals you have been examining to adopt, based on an analysis of risk and expected performance.

Consider the case of Mattel Inc., the American toy company, which made news when it announced in 1998 that it intended to reduce its dependence on the U.S. market by doubling its international sales in the next five years.[1] To do this, the company would begin to design and produce toys for individual foreign markets, rather than simply adapting U.S. products. The organization structure would be changed to give more prominence to international activities, and bonus incentives would be tied to international growth targets.

Mattel's plan was ambitious, and would definitely require new resources, new management preferences, and the development of new organizational capabilities. By way of example, let us focus on one aspect of the challenge facing Mattel: hiring non-American employees, and then learning to manage a more diverse, multicultural organization. In all likelihood, it will not be so difficult for Mattel to hire the needed new resources, in the form of people who understand foreign markets, foreign business practices, and speak languages other than English. But Mattel's American employees will now need to learn to work effectively with those of other nationalities, and vice versa. The company will also have to learn to create attractive international career paths and manage employees on foreign assignments. Developing the ability to work effectively across cultures usually takes some time. Will Mattel be able to develop this new organizational capability in the time available? Clearly management is betting that it will—but nothing is certain. In this particular example we would judge that developing the new organizational capability (the ability to work across cultures) will prove more difficult than the challenge of finding the new resources.

There are, of course, many other types of organizational capabilities. In Chapter 1 we mentioned 3M's outstanding ability to innovate, a capability which has underpinned the company's strategy for the past 85 years. In other businesses the prized capability is to produce at the lowest cost. Aluminum companies, for example, routinely prepare and study histograms showing the relative cost positions of each of their smelters and those of competitors all over the world. The perpetual challenge is to find ways to move down the cost curve. Such an emphasis is common in industries in which the price of the end product is beyond the control of any individual player.

Another capability (see Table 7.1) that has gained prominence in recent years is speed. Western firms with Japanese competitors have become aware of just how slow, in comparison, some of their processes are. American auto companies realized that the time to develop new models had to be cut by 50 percent. Jack Welch, CEO of General Electric, proclaimed that "speed, simplicity, and self confidence"[2] were to become the hallmarks of GE businesses, and many other companies have tried to follow suit. Welch also highlighted "boundarylessness,"[3] meaning the ability to work effectively across boundaries inside and outside the organization. Many companies are working to develop this capability, but finding it difficult.

Capabilities such as those shown in Table 7.1 do not exist in isolation in an organization. They are based on the behaviour of your employees, which is in turn influenced and supported by the culture of the organization. We have illustrated these relationships in Figure 7.2. In this diagram, which is the basis for much of this chapter, we have also included three organizational leverage points which both support your existing culture, behaviour, and capabilities and act as your potential levers for change. As we shall discuss later, if you want to develop new capabilities you will need to change the behaviour and culture of your organization. These three leverage points are the means you have to do so.

TABLE 7.1
Examples of Organizational Capabilities

Innovation

The capacity to stimulate and support strategies based on new ideas. Perhaps the creation of new markets, new products, new processes.

Prominent example: 3M.

Productivity

The capacity to stimulate and support strategies based on cost efficiency and price.

Prominent example: British Petroleum.

Speed

The capacity to stimulate and support strategies based on speed. Perhaps to be first to market with new products, first to develop new technologies, first to gain government approvals, or to offer fast response to customer needs.

Prominent example: ABB.

Cross-Cultural Effectiveness

The capacity to stimulate and support strategies based on unusually effective cooperation between employees of different cultures. The ability to gain a competitive edge by taking advantage of cultural diversity within the firm.

Prominent example: Nestlé.

Cross-Unit Synergies

The capacity to stimulate and support strategies which require seamless cooperation and support between different units within the company. Perhaps cooperation between business units, functional units, geographic regions.

Prominent example: Disney.

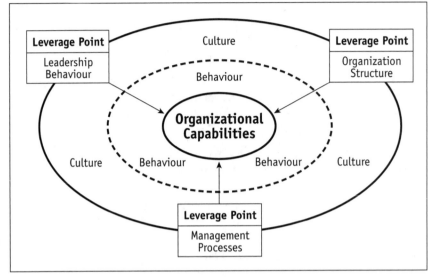

FIGURE 7.2
The
Organizational
Capabilities
Model

Later in the chapter we will ask you to identify the changes in behaviour and culture that you would need to bring about in order to develop new organizational capabilities in your business. To help visualize such relationships, we have provided some examples in Table 7.2. Further examples are provided in the following sections in which we take a closer look at behaviour and culture.

TABLE 7.2
Organizational Capability, Behaviour, and Culture

Organizational Capability	Related Behaviour	Supporting Cultural Belief
• the ability to be more often right than wrong with major capital investments	• thorough data collection, thorough analysis	• we would rather be right than quick
• quick and appropriate response to customer requests	• decision making close to the customer	• we believe in delegation of responsibility and authority
• the ability to be a low cost producer	• focusing on activities that add financial value	• everything comes down to money
• ability to innovate	• financial and moral support for fledgling projects	• new product ideas are precious

BEHAVIOUR

When we speak of behaviour, we are talking of readily observable behaviour, not aspects of people's actions that one would need to be a trained psychologist to notice. When managers refer to the behaviour of others in their firm, they are generally thinking of how much energy they put into various aspects of their job, how they manage their subordinates, how much attention they give to external issues, how they relate to one another, and so on. One senior manager discussing the behaviour of executives who reported to him stated the following:

> *All of my managers are pressed for time. Everyone has more things on their "to do" list than they can possibly get around to doing. So for me the essence of behaviour is not about what time people get to work or how they dress, it is about what items come to the top of the priority list. Given all of the things that a manager could choose to spend his or her time on, which will they actually choose? If I am going to bring about change here, I have to begin by changing the things that come to the top of people's priority lists.*

Clearly the priorities of senior managers are an important element of behaviour, but you will have to cast a wider net to capture all of the key behaviour changes that would be necessary to develop a new organizational capability. A group of senior managers in a global chemical company, for example, wanted to develop new capabilities to support a move from commodity to specialty chemicals, and they went to some lengths to describe the behavioural changes that would be required. The four capabilities they were seeking were (1) the ability recognize and assess changes in the external environment in a more timely fashion; (2) the ability to make better strategic choices—particularly a willingness to say *no* to more projects; (3) the ability to meet quality and delivery promises made to customers; and (4) an enhanced ability to understand where they were, and were not, performing well. The behaviours required to support these capabilities are listed in Table 7.3, alongside descriptions of current behaviour. Collectively they referred to the process of developing the new behaviours and capabilities as "getting more market focused."

The change in behaviour that these managers wanted to achieve in their company was going to be difficult, and they knew it. The problem, as one of them expressed it, was that

> *We have a strong culture, which has resulted from our successful history, and it supports the current behaviour. We knew that if we were to change behaviour in anything more than a very temporary way, we were going to have to find a way to change our culture. I think many long established companies face the same problem.*

TABLE 7.3
Inwardly Focused and Market-Focused Behaviour

Internally Focused Behaviour	Market-Focused Behaviour
Assessing the External Environment	
We are absorbed by internal issues and indifferent to market-based information.	We need to be driven by external challenges, taking pains to acquire and share market information.
Making Strategic Choices	
We think of internal political realities when decision making.	We need to make choices in line with external realities and internal capabilities, based on judgments of future performance.
Achieving Operational Excellence	
We work in boxes and guard boundaries. Kick disputes upstairs.	We need to operate as a team. Solve disputes on the spot.
Assessing Performance	
We measure progress by internal standards.	We need to measure progress by external standards.

CULTURE

An organization's culture, by which we mean the shared beliefs and expectations that managers have about the way the organization should operate, can have a major impact on the behaviour of everyone in the organization, and thus on its capabilities. In an organization with a strong culture, those beliefs will be widely shared and strongly held.

As part of your organizational snapshot you should identify the key elements of your company's culture. Do not be concerned if you cannot be particularly precise. One writer described corporate cultures as having "the ephemeral qualities of flame or fog. You know they're there; you know they're real; but you can't grab hold of them or even describe them very well . . . ."[4] We mentioned earlier 3M's continued capacity for innovation; here are some phrases used by 3M employees that capture important elements of the 3M culture:[5]

"Listen to anyone with an original idea, no matter how absurd it may sound at first."

"Encourage; don't nitpick. Let people run with an idea."

"Hire good people and leave them alone."

"Encourage experimental doodling."

"Give it a try, and quick."

Try to make a similar list to describe your own company's culture, particularly those elements of it which are most strongly held. It will be critical, later in your analysis, that you be able to tell the difference between new organizational capabilities your culture could support and those it could not. If a strategic proposal would require capabilities that you judge would fit well with the existing culture, you will probably be confident of your ability to implement it. If this is not the case, you will need to be cautious.

In the early 1990s Sir David Simon at British Petroleum was trying to create a new culture in which all employees would understand that "everything comes down to money." In doing so, he was up against a very strongly entrenched culture. He recounted a conversation between himself and a worker on an oil rig:

> I ask: "How much money do you make?" An employee will reply: "I can tell you how much oil we produce." I say: "Yes, but I am not interested in how much oil you produce, this is a factory for me. Where's the money?" Oil is only relevant in terms of money for shareholders, not in terms of barrels. That's very important. It's part of the change that can be implied by the direction the board takes. The board can say: "We want this to be a performing culture, we want this culture to understand much more about the commercial than the technical merits of the business." Those are very deep-seated cultural issues.[6]

Needless to say, a "deep-seated" culture, as Sir David put it, can be a real asset if it supports the behaviour and capabilities required by your current or proposed strategy. If your culture is strongly held but inappropriate, however, it will be a major hindrance.

Before leaving the topic of culture, we must emphasize that an organization's culture not only pushes "inward" (in Figure 7.2), impinging on behaviour and capabilities, but also has an "outward" force, influencing the choices that managers make about the organization structure, management processes, and the leadership behaviour of senior managers in the organization. We will examine this outward influence in more detail when we discuss the judgments you will make about your firm's ability to develop new capabilities, but, to give one example now, consider the choices that managers make when making hiring and promotion decisions.

There is no doubt that hiring and promotion decisions are a vital aspect of corporate life, and have a major impact on the collective behaviour and capabilities of the corporation. So how are such decisions made? In many companies, new employees are hired because they look like they would "fit in," and they are promoted once it is clear they are competent, and are "our kind of manager." Herb Kelleher, CEO of Southwest Airlines, one of *the* success stories of the past decade in the American airline business, expresses the views of many CEOs in the following statement:

We'll take the person with less experience if he or she has the values we are looking for . . . . We look for attitudes. We'll train you on whatever you need to do, but the one thing that we can't do is change inherent attitudes in people . . . . Part of the purpose of the probationary period is to deter- mine that. You may be an exceptional performer, but incompatible with our culture here. It doesn't mean there is anything wrong with you, there is just not a match.[7]

Clearly such decisions reinforce and support the existing culture. If that cul- ture supports the capabilities that you need for the challenges that lie ahead, you are in great shape. If not, you may face a major challenge.

We are now ready to turn to the analytical steps outlined in Figure 7.1. As you work your way through these steps you may wish to return to Figure 7.2 from time to time, as your judgments about the relationships depicted there will play a crucial role in your assessment as to whether, and how, your orga- nization could develop needed new capabilities.

STEP 1: IDENTIFY REQUIRED ORGANIZATIONAL CAPABILITIES

The first step in deciding if your organization is likely to prove capable of im- plementing a new strategy is to break the strategy into its four component parts, and identify the capabilities needed for each. We suggest that you do this by preparing a table like Table 7.4. The difficulty you are likely to have in doing this is that your analysis will be hypothetical; meaning that you are guessing at what it would take to implement a strategy that you have never, in fact, imple- mented. There are several things to keep in mind as you do this:

Be As Specific As You Can About the Capabilities That You Will Need If your value proposition to customers, for example, is going to include "out- standing customer service," you will need the capability to deliver that. But what does "outstanding" actually mean? Remember that the quality of your service will be judged by customers, not by you, and their standard of comparison will be the service offered by others. So do some benchmarking. You may discover that "outstanding" means that you would need to offer 24-hour turnaround to a client needing repairs to a piece of equipment, anywhere in the world. That is a clear demand, and later you will have to assess whether or not you can develop the organizational capability to meet it. "Outstanding" is too vague to be useful.

Cast a Wide Net When making your capability assessment ask people from dif- ferent areas in your company to participate—not just one level in the hierarchy,

TABLE 7.4
Identifying Required Capabilities

Objective	Required Capability
Implement New Goals	What are the most critical organizational capabilities required by the goals of the new strategic proposal? (For example, an ability to stimulate and manage a faster rate of growth.)
Implement New Value Proposition	What are the most critical organizational capabilities required by the value proposition of the new strategic proposal? (For example, the ability to respond to customer requests within 24 hours.)
Implement New Product-Market Focus	What are the most critical organizational capabilities required by the product-market focus of the new strategic proposal? (For example, an ability to move aggressively into international markets.)
Implement New Core Activities	What are the most critical organizational capabilities required by the key activities of the new strategic proposal? (For example, the ability to manage outsourced activities, or to establish joint ventures.)
Close Resource Gaps	What are the most critical organizational capabilities that will be required to close the resource gaps that you identified in your resource analysis of the strategic proposal?
Close Preferences Gaps	What are the most critical organizational capabilities that will be required to close the management preferences gaps that you identified in your preferences analysis of the strategic proposal?

and not just one functional area. And ask outsiders: customers, suppliers, and others who know the market that you are proposing to enter.

As you can see from the bottom two rows of Table 7.4, you will also need organizational capabilities to close the resource gaps and preferences gaps that you identified earlier, and these should be included in your analysis. This may not be obvious at first glance, so consider the following examples.

Let us say that the strategic proposal that you are considering would require more research and development effort in particular new product areas. You do not have the resources to do this—in your earlier analysis you identified this as an important resource gap. When looking at ways of closing the gap, your first inclination was to hire more researchers, but for financial reasons that was not possible. The solution you came up with was to find a way to cut spending earlier on projects that are ultimately not going to be successful, and to divert the funds to ongoing projects. This action will close the resource gap, but it will require a new organizational capability, as making an early identification of products that will ultimately fail is easier said than done. The capability has two parts: the ability to collect and assess new information; and the ability to make unpopular decisions that will be resisted by the researchers involved, with less solid information (because the decision is being made earlier) than was previously the case.

Identifying the organizational capabilities that would be required to close management preference gaps may require somewhat more subtle judgments. As we pointed out in Chapter 6, serious management preference gaps mean that there is conflict between managers. Adopting the strategic proposal you are considering would bring this conflict into the open, perhaps because some managers support it and other do not, or perhaps because it would mean that two organizational units would have to work closely together to make it succeed, and you know there would be conflict between the managers involved. The needed organizational capability is a willingness to acknowledge such conflict and deal directly with it. In many organizations strategy changes which would necessitate dealing with such conflicts are instinctively avoided—senior managers know that they do not have the capability to deal with the tension and stress that would result.

STEP 2: IDENTIFY CAPABILITY GAPS

Now that you have identified the organizational capabilities that you would need to implement the strategic proposal you are considering, you need to compare those capabilities with the capabilities that you already have, and identify the most significant gaps. This is a relatively straightforward and focused exercise because you have already identified the capabilities that really matter. The question is whether or not you have these capabilities and, if not, the nature and size of the gaps that need to be filled.

As you do this, be careful to avoid flattering assessments of your capabilities. Again we suggest involving a number of people in this exercise, from different functional areas and levels in the hierarchy. Be honest; this is no place for wishful thinking. Remember that capabilities are relative. There is no use comparing yourself to the worst performer in the industry if you are going to be competing head-to-head against the best. On the other hand, although the primary purpose of this exercise is to identify capability gaps, do be on the lookout for unique organizational capabilities that you possess which could form the basis of a new strategy others would find difficult to copy.

In Table 7.5 we have included one task that we have not yet discussed, and that is the determination of the actions that would be required to close the organizational capability gaps that you have identified. It is to this major challenge that we now turn.

STEP 3: DEVELOP NEW ORGANIZATIONAL CAPABILITIES

Your capability gap analysis will give you a pretty clear picture of the new organizational capabilities that you need to develop. How to do it is much less straightforward, and as the annals of business failure suggest, fraught with danger. We are all familiar with companies that embarked on well-intentioned reorganizations that did more harm than good, managers who made changes in compensation systems to induce new behaviour that led to unanticipated dysfunctional consequences, and new strategies that never got off the ground because everyone ignored the "not very inspirational" messages coming from head office about how we are "all going to do things differently from now on." You are going to need to make some fine judgment calls about the best way to encourage people in your organization to change their behaviour as required to develop the new capabilities that you need.

To begin, we refer back to Figure 7.2 and the three leverage points which, as we said then, are your potential tools for developing new capabilities. For ease of exposition we discuss these sequentially and individually, while recognizing that the interaction and consistency between the three is important. The three leverage points are (1) *organization structure,* which captures the way you have grouped people around tasks and established reporting relationships, as reflected in your firm's organization chart; (2) *management processes,* which are the processes that you use to manage the company and the people in it; and (3) *leadership behaviour,* which is the way senior managers lead the company.

TABLE 7.5
Identifying Organizational Capability Gaps and Required Action

Required Organizational Capabilities	Existing Organizational Capabilities	Capability Gaps	Action to Close Gaps
Derived from strategic proposal, resource gap analysis, preferences gap analysis	Derived from observation	Derived from comparison of first two columns	Changes in organization structure, management processes, leadership behaviour required to develop new organizational capabilities

ORGANIZATION STRUCTURE

Your organization structure is reflected in your organization chart. It shows how you have chosen to group the people in your organization and assign responsibilities. The way you have grouped people will make some tasks easier to carry out than others. This is a natural result of the fact that people working closely together will get to know one another's strengths and weaknesses, learn to trust each other's judgments, and will naturally focus on whatever task they have in common, be that developing a new video game or serving customers who are complaining about their recently purchased automobile.

No matter what choices you have made, your structure will not support every capability that you would like to have in the organization. There are always trade-offs to be made. Generally speaking, information and influence run most easily in a vertical direction, up and down whatever hierarchy you have created. The management challenge is usually to develop horizontal links, across the organization. These will be outside the formal reporting relationships, and typically do not happen without active encouragement. Thus, if you have organized by product division (to be discussed) your challenge will be to get people in different product groups to communicate and cooperate. If you have organized in geographic units the challenge will be to get sharing of experience between geographic regions.

In the following sections we have described some of the most commonly used organization structures, and the capabilities that they are likely to enhance. As a way of illustrating these basic structures, we have presented in Figure 7.3 the hypothetical case of a publishing company organized with a functional structure, a product organization, a geographic organization, and as a matrix. We refer to this example in each of the following sections.

Functional Structure

The traditional organizational building block is the functional unit, which consists of people working together within the same business function—research, engineering, manufacturing, marketing, sales, service, and so on—reporting to a general manager. Only the general manager is responsible for profitability. Small companies typically have such a structure, and the general manager is the president of the company. Companies that grow while maintaining a narrow product line may stick with their functional structure, ending up with a worldwide functional organization. In the hypothetical publishing company of Figure 7.3, there would be a head of global manufacturing with responsibility for producing books, magazines, and newspapers; a global marketing department responsible for marketing these products around the world; and so on, each reporting to the chief executive.

A company with a functional structure is likely to be very good at coordinating activities and allocating resources within each function. Most of the

FIGURE 7.3
Basic Organization Structure (Partial)

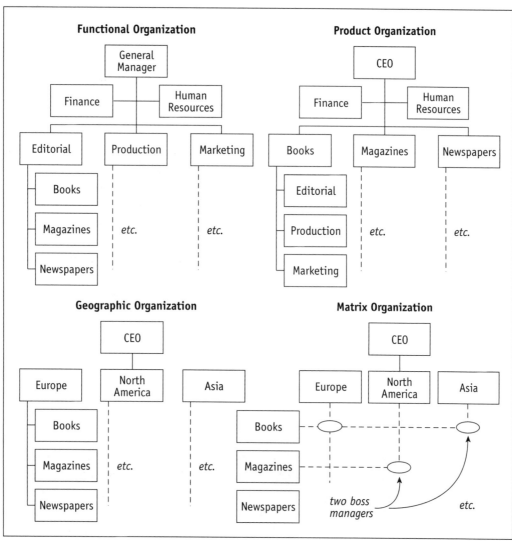

major oil companies, for example, have a global exploration department, which reviews opportunities all over the world, before deciding where to drill. When the Swiss pharmaceutical company Novartis was formed from the merger of Sandoz and Ciba-Geigy in 1996, senior management took the opportunity to get rid of geographically run research centres, each of which had had their own funding and research agenda.[8] Instead the company established seven therapeutic areas of research, each of which would have a global mandate. As the head of research put it, "science is not local; it's global." Now Novartis makes global decisions with respect to the amount it wants to spend in each of the seven therapeutic areas; previously the decision was how much it wanted to spend in various areas of the world.

As these examples suggest, a global functional structure has many benefits to offer a company that is producing a standardized product for sale around the world. There one could expect to find such things as compact discs, a "world car," or computer software packages for global adoption, such as Windows 98, being created, produced, and marketed in a global functional structure. This would offer the best opportunities for efficiency in worldwide design, production, marketing, and distribution. A global functional structure also offers the opportunity for low-cost manufacturing, as world-scale production facilities can be created, and then managed centrally, giving opportunities for optimal, raw-material sourcing, production scheduling, and so on.

The potential disadvantages of a worldwide functional structure may be a lack of sensitivity to local markets, slow decision making, and poor coordination between the functional areas. The problem may be that the engineers don't talk to the manufacturing people, the manufacturing people don't talk to marketing, and marketing does not talk to the sales organization. The result is beautifully engineered products that manufacturing cannot produce and customers are not willing to pay for, creative marketing plans that bear no relationship to the product range that manufacturing can deliver, and so on. The challenge for companies with large functional organizations is to find formal and informal methods of horizontal communication between the functions, so that information passing between, say, an engineer working on a new product design and a marketer planning its introduction does not have to go to the top of the hierarchy, across, and back down.

Most managers who are moving away from large functional structures say that they are doing so to enhance the speed and responsiveness of their organizations. They argue that by breaking the organization into smaller units they will get decision making closer to the customer, and faster. The usual resistance to such a change comes from the heads of the functional units, who see themselves as likely to lose status and power in such a transition.

Product Organization

If a company with a functional structure grows by adding new products, the structure will become awkward, as within each functional area there will be groups of people associated with each product, with different knowledge, different challenges, and different priorities. This would be true, for example, if our publishing company began life as a book publisher, then added magazines and then newspapers. In the early days of a new product's life it is likely to suffer from a lack of attention, as most people in the functional structure will be preoccupied with the original product, which in all probability will be providing the bulk of the company's revenue. To avoid such problems, at a certain point a second product division will be formed around the new product. It will be a profit centre, headed by a general manager who will report to the CEO. If the product divisions do not need their own legal function, personnel department, or finance function, these groups may report in at a corporate level, as shown in Figure 7.3.

The advantage of a product organization is the focus that it gives to each product line in the company. The performance of each product area is visible, and resources can be allocated to each. This clarity and focus comes at a cost, in contrast to the large functional structure. The product organization represents duplication, as you now have a general manager, a marketing manager, manufacturing manager, and so on, for each product group. This is why the decision as to when to split a existing division into two is not an obvious one. Companies that focus on innovation, like 3M, want a lot of care and attention given to new products, and as a result tend to create new product divisions early.

The potential disadvantage of a product organization is that the divisions may not share knowledge and learn from one another. This may or may not be important, depending on the similarity of their technology, customer base, or the geographic markets that they are serving. Let us say, for example, that our publishing company had three worldwide product divisions (books, magazines, newspapers) each of which operated in Brazil. The result could be three senior managers located in Brazil, in different cities, not sharing any overheads, not coordinating their paper purchases or local employment practices, and not working together in representing their interests to various government agencies. The usual solution is to establish an informal horizontal liaison between the businesses, or to appoint a country president. The latter is a somewhat thankless job, however, as such presidents have very little power. Managers within the country report to managers in their product division elsewhere in the world, not to the president. As one disgruntled ex-country president recently put it, "I came in each morning to raise the flag and turn on the lights, and that was about it."

There is also a danger that customers will not be happy with a product-based organization, if they are buying from more than one product division. They may prefer a single point of contact, a single invoice, and a sales representative who understands all of their needs. One solution, described in some detail by Jay Galbraith,[9] is a front-back hybrid organization in which the "back" of the company (production, for example) may be organized into different product units, to achieve efficiency, but the sales activity is bundled such that only one sales person calls on a given customer. Such a structure has the potential to give manufacturing focus, while reducing sales force duplication and at the same time giving customers what they want.

Geographic Structure

In a geographically organized company the level below the CEO comprises executives who are responsible for various areas of the world. Each has the responsibility to maximize financial results within that area, for all of the firm's products. Nestlé's manager for Germany, for example, is responsible for the total company results in the country, and it is up to him or her to decide how much attention is to be given to frozen foods, chocolate, coffee, pet food, and so on, within that market.

Managers and employees at all levels in geographically based organizations get to know their area well. They know the politics, the changing tastes of consumers, the local competitors, the labour market, and so on. Thus, a geographically based organization is likely to be skilled at tailoring products and marketing approaches to local conditions. So if your strategy is to adapt your product and marketing approach to local tastes (as is common in the food industry, for example) a geographically based structure may be the way to go.

A geographic structure may also help if you are trying to learn how to do business in areas of the world that are new to you. For example, in a geographically based organization there would likely be a general manager for China, to whom the heads of all the company's businesses in the country would report. This would maximize the opportunity for learning among the businesses, and allow the company to have a "China strategy" which would not be possible if each businesses reported into a separate worldwide organization. Any contact between the businesses within the country would be at their own initiative, and not naturally fostered by the organization structure.

The disadvantage of geographic structures is that they do not naturally lend themselves to global efficiency. The management team in every country usually has a reason why its product, marketing approach, advertising copy, and so on, need to be different. Some of these claims may be entirely justified, but others may just be a bid for local autonomy, to keep decision making within the country unit and away from head office.

In the past decade there has been a clear movement towards product structures, at the expense of the traditional geographic structure. Procter & Gamble announced in mid 1998 that it would abandon its long-standing regional structure of four geographic divisions, and create three new global product divisions: laundry detergents, diapers, and shampoos. Each global business unit will have full profit responsibility and "all the resources it needs to understand consumer needs in its product area and to develop innovative products to meet those needs."[10] The company plans to double sales revenue in the next 10 years, and to do that, it judges that it needs to get new products to market in half the time that it currently takes. In our terms the new capability that P&G is trying to develop is clear, and the reorganization is one of the tools designed to bring that about.

Matrix

Matrix structures are used by companies that do not want to put one element of organization, say product line or geography, in a superior position to others. Rather than having one primary organizing logic, they have two, or possibly more, which results in a number of managers reporting to multiple bosses, as illustrated in Figure 7.3. Thus, a marketing manager located in France may report to the president of the French subsidiary, and to a vice president of a worldwide marketing function for the product line that he or she is selling. Managed properly, such a structure encourages managers to pay attention to both local needs and worldwide product strategies.

One historically successful user of a worldwide matrix organization was Asea Brown Boveri (ABB). This Zurich-based multinational operates in 50 business areas and 1100 local geographic regions. For 10 years the company employed a matrix structure in which the presidents of the 1100 companies reported to two bosses—to a business area boss and to the president of the national company. Percy Barnevik, CEO of this 240 000-employee company, commented on the rationale for the firm's matrix organization:

> ABB is an organization with three internal contradictions. We want to be global and local, big and small, radically decentralized with centralized reporting and control.... That's where the matrix comes in. It allows us to optimize our business globally and maximize performance in every country in which we operate.[11]

Offsetting these potential advantages, however, is the fact that matrix organizations are extremely complex, and tend to be slow moving. The major difficulty is the ambiguity that arises from managers reporting to multiple bosses. Responsibility and authority are diffused, and power balances are not as clear cut as they are in straightforward hierarchical organizations. One study concluded: "If you do not really need it, leave it alone. There are easier ways of managing companies."[12] Goran Lindahl, who took over as CEO from Barnevik in 1997 seemed to agree, and the company soon moved to a straightforward product-based organization. Lindahl described the change as "an aggressive move aimed at greater speed and efficiency by further flattening and focusing the organization."[13] The age of the matrix organization may not be over, but it certainly seems to be in decline.

MANAGEMENT PROCESSES

During the past 10 years managers have become much more conscious of the processes by which their companies make decisions and get things done. Spurred in part by advances in information technology, which allow fast and inexpen-

127

sive communication inside and outside the company, many senior managers have tried to find ways to increase the speed of response in their organizations, while at the same time reducing costs and doing things more reliably. Here is Paul Allaire, the chairman and CEO of Xerox Corporation, explaining that it is possible, through redesigning processes, to increase customer satisfaction and reduce cost at the same time:

> *You can't redesign processes until you know what you're trying to do. What you're after is congruence among strategic direction, organization design, staff capabilities, and the processes you use to ensure that people are working together to meet the company's goals . . . . We wanted to be more customer focused but no less efficient. That, we found, is the magic of processes, you can have it both ways. A process orientation allows you to take huge amounts of cost out of the system while still improving customer satisfaction.[14]*

There are many types of management processes. For ease of exposition we focus here on three which generally have a major impact on a firm's capabilities: *decision-making processes, operating processes, and performance assessment and reward processes*. Decision-making processes are the routines and procedures that you go through for making the important decisions in your business: setting direction, determining objectives, allocating resources, deciding how to serve customers, and so on. Operating processes are the processes that create, produce, and deliver your products and services, including things such as your product development process, order fulfillment process, after-sales service process, and the like.[15] Performance measurement and reward processes are the ways in which you measure the performance of businesses and people, and reward them. In Table 7.6 we have provided examples of how you might change processes in each of these areas to develop a new organizational capability.

Decision-Making Processes

Whether we are talking of multi-billion-dollar acquisition decisions or a hotel clerk deciding how to deal with an irate customer, decision-making processes are of vital importance to every organization. Companies trying to develop new capabilities to support a new strategy often find that they need to learn to make decisions faster, better, or both. "Better" in this context means decisions that support the company's strategy and when viewed with hindsight will prove to have been successful.

When considering ways to change their decision-making processes, companies often focus on who is involved in particular decisions, what information they have, and how they actually make decisions. To take one example, consider the case of SmithKline Beecham.

The issue facing SmithKline Beecham (SB), a major pharmaceuticals company, was one that confronts many large organizations. The firm needed to make vital decisions about funding new drug-development projects, but the information needed to make those decisions came primarily from the project champions who were, in fact, competing for available development funds. There could be 20 projects under review at any given time, with more than half a billion dollars in investment at stake. The information presented may not be objective, and there was a suspicion that presentation skills may count for more than high quality analysis. But because the difference between good and bad decisions was potentially hundreds of millions of dollars in lost contribution, the company decided the problem was too important to ignore.

In 1993 SB set about to improve their resource allocation decision process. The details of how this was done are described elsewhere[16]; let us just say that this was not a trivial task. The project created controversy and debate in many areas of the company, and two years passed before the new process was fine-tuned and well accepted in the organization. In the words of Paul Sharpe and Tom Keelin, who were centrally involved in the project, "we learned that by tackling the soft issues around resource allocation, such as information quality, credibility, and trust, we had also addressed the hard ones: how much we should invest and where we should invest it."[17]

TABLE 7.6
Changing Management Processes to Develop New Capabilities

New Capability to Be Developed	Decision-Making Processes	Operational Processes	Performance Assessment and Reward Processes
e.g., **Faster Response to Customer Concerns**	Move customer-related decision making lower in the organization: closer to the customer.	Establish work routines that cut across functional boundaries.	Collect measures of customer satisfaction, as well as internal measures such as speed of response to customer requests.
e.g., **Increase Flow of New Products to Markets**	Make it hard to kill new product ideas early in their life.	Reduce the time to market by converting sequential processes to parallel processes.	Monitor the percentage of revenues or profits produced from new products in each business.
e.g., **Ability to Create Synergy Between Businesses**	Involve corporate level executives in major decisions to ensure potential synergies are not ignored.	Create cross-unit information flows and joint execution of projects.	Monitor cross-business initiatives.

Operating Processes

Operating processes govern the way that your employees work together to create, produce, and deliver products or services that your customers value. Generally, such processes work well if they are contained within a small organizational unit in a single location. Problems often arise, however, when coordination is required between larger units located in different places. The marketing group may make promises to customers that manufacturing cannot deliver; perhaps engineering designs products that manufacturing cannot produce at a reasonable cost; or the sales force in the West offers prices and conditions that are inconsistent with those in the East, and so on.

The new capabilities that many companies want to develop require closer coordination between organizational units than they have traditionally had. A global customer may be demanding seamless service around the world. Another customer may want to see only a single sales representative from the company, who represents a number of business units. Or perhaps the goal is cost reduction, and the links between product design and manufacturing, for example, have to become much tighter.

To increase cross-unit cooperation you may use informal mechanisms such as rotating personnel between the units where cooperation is desired, placing the units in the same physical location, holding frequent interdepartmental meetings, parties, and so on. If such measures are insufficient, the next step is to create more formal horizontal work groups, such as a new product development team, that cut across departments. Performance measurement and reward systems (to be discussed subsequently) can also be tailored to promote cross-unit cooperation.[18]

An organization that has done an excellent job of creating new capabilities in the past decade by fostering close cooperation between its component parts is the Walt Disney Company. Disney's intent is to create each year a core property that every unit in the company can use to generate profit, leveraging on the "character" produced and the Disney name. *The Lion King*, released in 1994, is a prime example. This movie, costing a reported $50 million to produce, brought in more than $750 million in box-office receipts in its first year, a clear success in itself, but was able to bring in more than *double* that amount from sales of home videos, books, music, TV rights, and licensing fees for merchandising of everything from toys to pajamas.

To create this capability, Michael Eisner, then CEO of Disney, created a vice president of synergy whose job was to ensure that each of Disney's nine business units were aware of what the others were up to, and that all synergistic possibilities were fully explored. In addition to the synergy group at head office, there were also synergy representatives in each business unit. Two or three times a year, senior managers met from around the world to present and discuss plans—and each group was expected to present initiatives that involved other units of the company. Synergistic initiatives were also expected in everyone's business plans, and were explicitly rewarded at bonus time.[19]

Few companies have been able to create such strong bonds across units, but many are trying. The trick is to create processes that will encourage useful cross-unit cooperation, without blurring the responsibility that managers feel for the performance of their own unit. "Yes, my own group's results are down, but look what I did for a sister division" is not a phrase that corporate managers want to hear.

Performance Assessment and Reward Processes

Many managers who want employees to behave differently change the performance assessment and reward processes in their organization. This seems a logical step, but it often leads to unintended consequences. Consider, for example, the commonly expressed desire to increase the level of teamwork in an organization, and its logical corollary, that employees should be paid on a team basis rather than on individual incentives. The case of Levi Strauss is a reminder to managers everywhere of just how careful one must be when trying to change behaviour by changing assessment and reward processes.[20]

In an industry where low wages and poor working conditions are common, Levi has prided itself on being an exception. It made a concentrated effort to pay its workers well, and at the same time keep plants operating in the United States when many companies were having jeans made in low-cost offshore locations. In 1992, in a bid to raise productivity, lower costs, and reduce repetitive strain injuries, Levi moved from its individual piece-rate pay system to a team-based approach in which workers would be paid on the output of their team of 10 to 35 people. The teams would be self-managed, and decide for themselves how to organize their work.

The result was a disaster on a number of dimensions. Fights constantly broke out within teams as faster workers berated slower ones for dragging down the group performance. The average pay of the faster workers declined, yet Levi's costs increased, as less productive workers were better off under the new scheme. Morale plummeted, and so did productivity. In 1997 the company, still unable to regain its former cost levels, announced the closure of ten plants in the United States, and the layoff of 6000 employees, one third of its U.S. workforce.

Our suggestion is that you be very cautious in assuming that new capabilities can be developed solely by changing performance assessment and rewards. Most employees work for more than money; they also want praise, encouragement, opportunity to grow, and fairness in rewards, to name but a few. In fact, you may want to avoid hiring people who are only interested in money. As Jeffery Pfeffer points out by way of example in his article "Six Dangerous Myths About

Pay,"[21] Tandem Computer, prior to its acquisition by Compaq, would not tell prospective employees what they would be paid if they joined the company, other than to say that salaries were competitive. The reasoning was that employees who come for money will leave for money, and they wanted new hires to join because they liked the work, the atmosphere, the people—the culture of the place.

If you decide that changing performance assessment and reward processes needs to be part of your program for changing behaviour and developing new capabilities, we suggest that you combine this change with other moves—in particular with changes in your own behaviour and that of other leaders in the firm. Otherwise, this risk of unintended consequences is very high.

LEADERSHIP BEHAVIOUR

Changes in organizational structure and management processes can be rather heavy, blunt tools for attempting to change behaviour. You may want to first try changing your own behaviour. If you are in a key position in the firm, this alone may have a dramatic impact. Ask yourself if your behaviour is representative of the behaviour that you believe is needed in the organization. Do you actively encourage your colleagues to adopt the required behaviour? In the vernacular, do you "walk the talk" and "talk the walk"? Have you made crystal clear, through your own behaviour and communication, the nature of the needed new behaviour?

An interesting example is provided by Quest, a former division of Unilever (now part of ICI) in the flavours and fragrances business.[22] Viktor Rensing, the CEO, believed that he could create a high-performance culture in the organization, based on a strong set of shared values, which would yield a permanent competitive edge. This was especially important in Quest, as the company had made 11 acquisitions in various countries between 1987 and 1994, and there appeared to be few, if any, shared values throughout the whole of the organization. As a first step, Rensing created a task force to take on the job of determining what Quest's key core values should be. They began by asking the five-person senior management team "what behaviour would you be most proud of in the year 2010 if it were typical of a Quest employee at that time?"

As the task force proceeded with identifying the core values of Quest, an unexpected thing happened. Richard Sweeney, who was leading the project, decided that proceeding in the usual way to advertise the new core values through catchy slogans, a video from the CEO, articles in the company newspaper, lucite paperweights with the values inside, and so on, did not make sense. If behaviour was going to change, he reasoned, it had to start at the top. The real message was not what Viktor Rensing and his colleagues said, it was what they did—how they behaved. The campaign was stopped, the task force disbanded, and the ball put squarely back in Rensing's court. After some soul-searching, the process was restarted, with intense personal discussions among the members of the top team, and behaviour did change. Then the process was cascaded downward through a series of workshops. Results improved dramatically over the next several years.

In Table 7.7 we have re-created the list of organizational capabilities that we used early in this chapter and suggested some starting points for thinking about how you might change your behaviour to drive other behavioural change throughout the organization.

Do You Have the Right Leaders?

As you work through your version of Table 7.7, you should also be thinking about the other leaders in the organization, and whether or not you have the right people in place. Do you make the right promotion decisions? Do you re-move the people that you should? In the first three years after taking over as CEO of AlliedSignal, Larry Bossidy changed 75 percent of the managers in the top 140 jobs in the company. Craig Weatherup, whom we will discuss in the next chapter, changed all but two of his 12 direct reports in a four-year change process at Pepsi USA.[23] You may judge that to develop new capabilities you are going to have to remove some of your current leaders.

TABLE 7.7
Organizational Capability and Leadership Behaviour

Organizational Capability	Behaviour Needed to Develop Required New Capabilities	Actual Behaviour	Needed Changes
Innovation	*e.g.* Could you do more to encourage innovation and experimentation? Are you innovative in your own activities? How do you handle well-intentioned failure?		
Productivity	*e.g.* Could you do a better job of asking questions that will lead others to focus more intensely on productivity issues? Do you focus on the key cost drivers often enough?		
Speed	*e.g.* Could you do more to demonstrate speed in your own behaviour and activities? Do you talk about speed as a success factor? Could you delegate in such a way as to speed up decision making or operating processes?		
Cross-Cultural Effectiveness	*e.g.* Could you improve your personal cross-cultural effectiveness? Do you encourage international careers? Could you do more to ensure that race-based bias is eliminated in your organization?		
Cross-Unit Synergies	*e.g.* Do you personally work well across organizational boundaries and encourage the same in others? Do you encourage group behaviour, information sharing?		

The related question is whether you should change your promotion criteria to get the leaders with the behaviour that you need. Bossidy commented:

> *We used to reward the lone rangers in the corner offices because their achievements were brilliant, even though their behaviour was destructive. That day is gone. We need people who are better at persuading than barking orders, who know how to coach and build consensus . . . . This has a big impact on how you think about who the "best" people are.*[24]

Larry Bossidy, like Jack Welch at General Electric, has established promotion criteria that take into account how a manager achieves results, as well as the results achieved. A manager who achieves results and does it "our way," meaning that he or she exhibits appropriate behaviour, is a star. One who does neither is out. The more interesting questions arise when the manager behaves well but does not produce (usually given a second chance) and, most difficult of all, when the manager produces results, but not with acceptable behaviour. Bossidy argues that such managers have to leave the company in spite of their results, because otherwise the whole drive for new behaviour will be undermined.

USING ALL THREE LEVERAGE POINTS

If your organization has a strong culture and deeply ingrained behaviour that you judge inappropriate, change is not going to be easy. To have any success, you will probably have to make changes in all three of the leverage points—structure, management processes, and leadership behaviour—that we have been discussing. It is important that the changes you make in each area send the same messages to employees about the desired new behaviour. It is extremely counterproductive, for example, to have a compensation system which rewards one type of behaviour, while managers are exhorting employees to do something different. Or if managers behave in one way, while suggesting that everyone else do something different.

Furthermore, consistency over time is critical. Frequent changes in structure, processes, or leadership behaviour will quickly breed employee cynicism, as they see "flavour-of-the-month" initiatives come and go. To return to an example of a company that seems to have its act together, we look again to 3M, and have produced in Table 7.8 some of the main features of its structure, processes, and leadership behaviour that work together to support its innovative capability.

STEP 4: ASSESS FEASIBILITY

At this point you have made your best estimate of the changes that would be required in your firm's structure, management processes, and leadership behaviour to implement the strategic proposal that you are examining. There are two

TABLE 7.8
3M's Innovative Capability

Leverage Point	Support for Innovation
Organization Structure	• "Grow and divide"; as businesses grow they are split into smaller units, each a profit centre with an autonomous management team.
Management Processes	• 30% of each year's sales must come from products less than 4 years old. Every business must meet this target. • "Pacing programs" were created to identify development programs that could make a major difference to the corporation, to receive priority funding. • "While products belong to businesses, technology belongs to the company," meaning that technology must be shared. This is done via numerous scientific forums and technology-sharing awards.
Leadership Behaviour	• "Thou shalt not kill a new product idea." • Acceptance of "well intentioned failure," to encourage risk taking. • Leaders must be capable of developing and managing teams. • "People will make mistakes, but they will not be as serious as the mistakes management will make if it tries to tell people exactly how to do their jobs." • Technical people are encouraged to spend up to 15% of their time on projects of their own choosing.

Sources: C. A. Bartlett and A Mohammed, *3M: Profile of an Innovating Company*, case 395-016, 1995. Boston: Harvard Business School. And www.3M.com.

questions that remain: (1) can these changes be made in the required time frame; and (2) will they produce the desired result? The answers are seldom an absolutely confident *yes* or a definitive *no*. They are more likely to be an estimate based on the nature and magnitude of the required changes in organizational capability (and hence behaviour and culture) that you are trying to bring about, and the extent to which various parts of the organization will embrace or resist the proposed changes.

You are likely to find that some of your managers will support the changes that you think are necessary, but others may resist. Recall that there is an arrow between management preferences and organization in the Diamond-E framework. This reflects the fact that managers may have strong individual preferences, and may not see the need for change the same way you do. This is a topic that we shall discuss in depth in the last two chapters of the book. For the moment, you should make a first estimate of likely support and resistance, and factor your thoughts into Table 7.9. You should complete such a table for each of the strategic proposals that you are considering.

This is also the time to think hard about the problem of "unintended consequences" that we discussed earlier. If you change some element of your management processes—the way you pay people, for example—will it really generate the behaviour change that you want? Or might it produce a rather different reaction? Remember the cautionary tale of Levi Strauss. If you are sure that your change will produce the desired result, record that in the fourth column of Table 7.9. Often the answer is a less confident one, and that lack of certainty needs to be considered when you are judging the feasibility of creating the required new capabilities in the time available.

Congratulations! You have now made it all the way around the Diamond-E and, assuming that you have more than one viable strategic proposal in hand, it is time to make a choice. That is the topic of the next chapter.

TABLE 7.9
Assessing Feasibility

Leverage Point	Nature and Magnitude of Required Change	Ability to Make Change in Time Required	Probability That the Change Will Bring About the Required Change in Capability	Overall Feasibility and Risk
Organization Structure				
Management Processes				
Leadership Behaviour				

 SUMMARY

In this chapter we discussed the penultimate step of the Diamond-E analysis, which is to decide if the strategic proposals that looked attractive during your environment, resource, and management preferences analyses could be implemented in the necessary time frame.

This analysis involves identifying the organizational changes that would be necessary in the firm's structure, management processes, and leadership behaviour to develop the capabilities you will need to support the new strategy. You must then make a crucial judgment regarding how likely it is that the proposed changes would have the desired result, and could be implemented in the given time frame. This assessment gives you a basis on which to weigh the risks against the benefits of the proposal.

If you are working through the Diamond-E analysis in the order that we have suggested, you may now have several attractive strategic proposals that have made it all the way through the drill. Choosing between them is the topic of the next chapter. If you have only one proposal, and it looks good, move directly to the last two chapters, which will assist you in building a change plan to implement your chosen strategy.

NOTES

1. Lisa Bannon, "Mattel Plans to Increase Global Sales," *Wall Street Journal Europe,* February 11, 1998, p. U9A.

2. Noel Tichy and Ram Charan, "Speed, Simplicity, and Self Confidence: An Interview With Jack Welch," *Harvard Business Review* (September–October 1989), p. 112.

3. R. Ashkenas, D. Ulrich, T. Jick, S. Kerr, *The Boundaryless Organization* (San Francisco: Jossey-Bass Publishers, 1995).

4. Harold J. Leavitt, *Corporate Pathfinders* (New York: Penguin Books, 1987), p. 16.

5. J. C. Collins and Jerry Porras, *Built to Last* (London: Century Business, Random House, 1996), p. 152.

6. Manfred F. R. Kets de Vries, "Transforming the Corporate Mind-set at British Petroleum: An Interview With Sir David Simon and John Browne," INSEAD case study, 497-013-4, 1997, p. 10.

7. Walter Goldsmith and David Clutterbuck, *The Winning Streak Mark II* (London: Orion Business Books, 1997), p. 183.

8. L. M. Fischer, "How Novartis Became Number One," *Strategy and Business* (Second Quarter 1998), p. 70.

9. Jay R. Galbraith, *Designing Organizations: An Executive Briefing on Strategy, Structure, and Process* (San Francisco: Jossey-Bass Publishers, 1995), p. 89.

10. Richard Tomkins, "The What, Not the Where to Drive P&G," *Financial Times,* September 3, 1998, p. 16.

11. William Taylor, "The Logic of Global Business: An Interview With ABB's Percy Barnevik," *Harvard Business Review* (March–April 1991), p. 90.

12. S. Davis and D. R. Lawrence, *Matrix* (Reading, Mass.: Addison Wesley, 1977), p. vi.

13. *Financial Times,* August 13, 1998, p. 1.

14. David A. Garvin, "Leveraging Processes for Strategic Advantage," *Harvard Business Review* (September–October 1995).

15. D. A. Garvin, "The Processes of Organization and Management," *Sloan Management Review* (Summer 1998), p. 33.

16. Paul Sharpe and Tom Keelin, "How SmithKline Beecham Makes Better Resource Allocation Decisions," *Harvard Business Review* (March–April 1998), p. 45.

17. ibid., p. 57.

18. Jay Galbraith, *Designing Organizations*, Chapters 4 and 5.

19. For further details, see the Harvard Business School case series, Disney's "The Lion King" (A), (B),and (C), by Cate Reavis under the direction of Carin-Isabel Knoop and Professor Jeffery Rayport. 1998. Case numbers N9-899-041,-042 and -043.

20. R. T.King Jr., "Levi's Factory Workers Are Assigned to Teams, and Morale Takes a Hit," *Wall Street Journal*, Wednesday, May 20, 1998, p. 1.

21. Jeffery Pfeffer, "Six Dangerous Myths About Pay," *Harvard Business Review* (May–June 1998), p. 109.

22. Jim Dowd and Mary Schweinsberg, Quest Core Values (A) and (B), IMD case GM 648-649, 1997.

23. D. A. Garvin, "Leveraging Processes for Strategic Advantage," *Harvard Business Review* (September–October 1985), p. 83.

24. N. M. Tichy and R. Charan, The CEO As Coach: An Interview With AlliedSignal's Lawrence A. Bossidy, *Harvard Business Review* (March–April 1995).

STRATEGIC CHOICE

Now, at last, it is time to make a strategic choice. You may be in the happy position of having a very attractive strategic proposal to move forward with, or even several good possibilities from which to choose. On the other hand, you may have ended up with one or more uncertain propositions and you are faced with trying to decide whether you should go ahead or recycle yet again to see if you and your management team can come up with some better options.

Before making a decision, you need to pull together the most critical parts of your Diamond-E analysis on each proposal. We suggest a format for this in Table 8.1. Revisit each element of your work (strategy-environment, strategy-resources, strategy-management preferences, and strategy-organization) to identify the major uncertainties associated with each. Then indicate the best case, worst case, and most likely outcome in each area of uncertainty. As you do this, you might find that events or outcomes in one area are linked to those in another. Pay close attention, as this is the first time that you have explicitly looked for links *between* the different areas of your Diamond-E analysis. We call this *cross-category impact.* The assessment of cross-category impact is the last logical step in your strategic assessment.

By way of example, let us say that your strategic proposal is to enter a new area of business. You know that one of the firms already in this business is working on a new technology that could result in an improved product at lower cost. You are not sure, however, whether this technology will actually work or, if it does work, in what time frame the improved product could arrive on the market. You have considered various possibilities in your strategy-environment assessment. Your "best case" outcome is that the new technology is a total failure, and your "worst case" is that it is both more effective than expected, and arrives early.

The cross-category impact starts to emerge as you realize that if the new technology comes much earlier than expected you will have trouble raising the equity that you need to fund your entry into this business. Furthermore, your vice presidents of finance and engineering, who have been lukewarm about entering the new business from the start, might resist even more strongly, once they see the competitor's new product on the market, and not give the new strategy the support that it will require. Their lack of enthusiasm will be readily apparent to their subordinates, who will put tasks associated with the new entry low on their priority lists, and will not assign their best people to the new business area.

It is in this way that an external event, over which you have no control, might impinge on (1) your ability to raise new resources, (2) the likelihood that you will be able to change the management preferences of at least two key managers, and (3) your ability to marshal the organizational capabilities needed to support the new strategy. These are the types of linkages that you should be looking for as you prepare Table 8.1.

TABLE 8.1
Strategic Proposal Performance Projections

Diamond-E Relationship	Major Uncertainties	Worst Case	Most Likely	Best Case
Strategic Proposal One				
Strategy-Environment				
Strategy-Resources				
Strategy-Management Preferences				
Strategy-Organization				
Proposal One: Performance Projections				
Strategic Proposal Two				
Etc.				

The final step in completing Table 8.1 is to create performance projections for each strategic proposal. These do not need to be extremely detailed, but they should include the key profit and loss and balance sheet items, under best case, worst case, and most likely conditions.

At this point you should have a good feel for the potential risks and payoffs of each of your proposals. The choice is yours to make. Don't allow yourself to be paralyzed by risk. The challenge now is to balance the risks that you are taking against the enhanced performance that is likely to result. If you have followed the analysis that we have suggested thus far, you have done enough homework! It is time to make a decision. Remember that the biggest risk of all may be in making no decision, or deciding to wait for events to unfold.

To successfully implement your chosen strategy, you will need to initiate and manage change in your organization. You will need to determine the nature of the needed changes, the urgency for change, the support that will be available, and the resistance that you will face, and then determine best way forward. These are the topics to which we turn in the last two chapters.

STRATEGIC CHANGE: CHANGE AGENDA AND STARTING CONDITIONS

This chapter is the first of two dealing with the implementation of strategic change. To this point we have focused on identifying and assessing strategic problems and opportunities, and deciding what changes in strategy would be most beneficial for your business. Now we turn to action. How do you go about making the changes that are necessary to implement your new strategy?

There are many challenges and choices facing managers wishing to implement change. A common obstacle, for example, is that many people in the organization may not be ready for change. Thus, you might begin your change program by looking for some easy wins—small changes that will have a positive impact—to demonstrate that altering the usual way of doing things can be beneficial. On the other hand, you might judge that it makes more sense to tackle the big tough issues immediately.

You will also face the challenge of deciding who should lead the change process, and how it should be led. It is unlikely that you will try to drive your change program alone. But should you spend your time and energy working with people who are most likely to agree with your proposed changes, or focus on those most likely to resist? Then there is the question of management style. Some managers lead change in a top-down, directive style, whereas others are more participative. Which is right for your situation?

This chapter and the next will help you develop a change plan to address such questions, but be forewarned that there is no generic set of "right answers" to the questions that emerge when one is managing change.[1] An appropriate change plan for you and your business will be unique to your situation, reflecting your particular change needs, and the conditions in which you are launching your change program.

THE CHANGE PLAN

An overview of the steps for building a change plan is presented in Figure 9.1. In this chapter we discuss the first two: identifying the change agenda that has emerged from your Diamond-E analysis, and analyzing the starting conditions that will shape your program of change. These include assessing the urgency for change, the readiness of the organization to make the required changes, and your personal readiness to lead the change. In Chapter 10 we will discuss guidelines for action and your specific action plan for achieving change.

FIGURE 9.1

Creating a Change Plan

CHANGE AGENDA

At this point you have completed your Diamond-E analysis and chosen your preferred strategic option. In that analysis, you identified new resources, new organizational capabilities, and perhaps new management preferences that will need to be developed to implement your new strategy. You also determined how you might bring about the changes in behaviour that you need in order to develop those new organizational capabilities, through changes in the senior management behaviour, the company's management processes, organization structure, or the way in which you manage people.

As a first step in developing a change plan, we suggest that you collect the change needs identified in your Diamond-E analysis to prepare a change agenda, as shown in Table 9.1. To prepare such a chart, take the change needs that have emerged from each section of your Diamond-E analysis, separating those that will require behavioural change from those that will not, and list the organizational changes that you identified in the analysis of Chapter 7 that might bring about those behavioural changes.

We suggest this because behavioural changes are often the most difficult to achieve, and this difficulty is often underestimated. The dangerous assumption is that if something makes sense (well, at least to the people proposing it) then everybody will fall in line and change their ways of doing things to conform with the new demands. Unfortunately, this seldom happens as easily as anticipated. People don't fall into line, sometimes because they just don't have the understanding and the skills required, and sometimes because they perceive, accurately or not, that the changes are not in their best interests.

TABLE 9.1
Change Agenda

	Change Needs Identified in Diamond-E Analysis		
	Non-Behavioural Changes Required	Behavioural Changes Required	Potential Changes in Organization
Develop New Resources			
Change Management Preferences			
Develop New Organizational Capabilities			

ANALYSIS OF STARTING CONDITIONS

The first of the three categories of starting conditions shown in Figure 9.1 is the *urgency* for action—how clear and pressing are the forces driving the action that you have in mind? The second category deals with *organizational readiness*—who are the people who will be most involved in or affected by the change, and how ready are they to adopt and implement the prescribed changes? The third category has to do with your *personal readiness*—given the course of action being considered, how well-prepared and positioned are you to lead the process of change? We will discuss these starting conditions in order.

URGENCY FOR ACTION: THE CRISIS CURVE

Urgency refers to the pressure to implement the changes that you have in mind. Naturally, there will always be some urgency attached to these changes. But the degree of urgency will vary with the strategic performance of your business and the timing of the impact of the changing conditions. This relationship is demonstrated in the crisis curve of Figure 9.2, in which we have identified three categories of urgency ranging from the relatively low pressure of anticipatory conditions to the absolutely immediate demands of crisis change.

A useful way to think about the crisis curve is as follows. Imagine a business that is doing very well, with performance improving over time as shown on the left-hand side of the curve. As some of the managers of this business look ahead they suspect that significant changes are going to occur in the environment, but these changes are in the future and uncertain in their impact. To implement strategic change at this time would be an act of *anticipatory change*—management is acting in anticipation of future events.

Suppose that, for a variety of reasons, the management of the business does not act on the forecast changes and these changes start to have an effect.

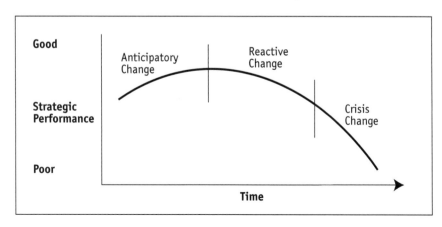

FIGURE 9.2
Urgency for Action: The Crisis Curve

Performance plateaus and then begins to deteriorate. To implement strategic change in this span of time would be an act of *reactive change*—management is reacting to current environmental pressures.

Suppose even further that management fails to act or to act effectively in response to the continuing development of external events. Performance deteriorates at an accelerating pace, leading to a point of crisis from which recovery is improbable. To implement strategic change as a business falls down this slope would be an act of *crisis change*.

Understanding where you are on the crisis curve provides some helpful cues about the management issues that you will have to tackle and helps you to focus your analysis on the precise starting conditions that you are dealing with. In Table 9.2 we have summarized the basic conditions of each change category and the management issues that are typically associated with them. We will review these characteristics in the following paragraphs. But first some words to elaborate the "strategic performance" measure.

The objective of measuring strategic performance, as we pointed out in Chapter 1, is to capture an accurate picture of the progress and position of a business in its markets. The most accessible measures for this purpose are those of revenue and profitability and for the most part these are satisfactory indicators. But remember that financial measures such as these are *lagging* indicators of the true progress and position of the business. Revenue, for example,

TABLE 9.2
Summary Characteristics of the Change Categories

	Anticipatory	Reactive	Crisis
Prevailing Conditions			
Strategic Performance	Healthy	Sliding	Critical
Need for Change	Uncertain	Becoming Clearer	Clear
Time Pressure	Little	Have to Get Started	Urgent
Internal Commitment for Change	Low	Mixed	High
Management Capability	High	Mixed	Low
Management Issues			
Strategic	Is Change Necessary?	Where to Start?	Achieving Rapid Pace of Change
Organizational	Lack of Commitment	Dealing With Resistors	Who to Rely On?
Personal	Credibility	Power	Links to Past

might continue to increase for some time after market share starts to fall because of underlying market growth, giving the illusion of progress. Similarly, market share can continue to increase for some time after the business has actually begun losing its position in the eyes of its customers, because of long-term commitments and inertia in purchasing habits and systems.

If you suspect that the financial indicators are indeed giving an optimistic reading of the true position of the business, it is very important to look beyond them to measures of market position and customer satisfaction. Otherwise the true urgency of the business situation will be misread.

Crisis Change

Crisis conditions are the most urgent and undeniable of the three change categories. The problems that you face are clear: an opportunity may be disappearing, sales may be in collapse, important customers may be cancelling orders, suppliers may be putting you on COD, a cash crunch may be imminent, banks may be on the brink of calling their loans, and so forth. Fast, focused, and decisive action is required. But this action may also be in vain; the business may have passed the point of no return.

In 1998, Weber and Beer analyzed the case of Asda (formerly Associated Dairies), one of England's largest supermarket chains.[2] Its board of directors had brought in 37-year-old Archie Norman to turn around the struggling business of 200 retail grocery stores. As is usually the case in crisis, the symptoms were visible both inside and outside the company, and Norman knew he was walking into a tough situation. "Turning around Asda was *the* big challenge in British retailing," he commented. "Here was a business that was a recognized failure."

When Norman arrived, the Asda chain had suffered from 10 years of poor management as it tried to move upmarket, away from its once well-established position at the low end of the market. The supermarket's traditional value-oriented customers were deserting it, employee morale was low, profits were declining, the company's stock price had fallen by 50 percent in three months, and it was in danger of defaulting on its debts, which were more than £1 billion.

Norman wasted no time, addressing Asda's senior management team at 9 AM on his first day on the job. Like most managers dropped into a crisis situation, he did not mince words: "Incremental change is not enough," he stated. "There are no sacred cows. Our number one objective is to secure value for the shareholders and to secure our trading future. I am not coming in with any magical solutions. I intend to spend the next few weeks listening and forming ideas for our precise direction."

He also declared that liquidity was critical, and every possible source of cash would be exploited to the full. In addition, there would be a reorganization to shorten reporting lines to the stores, to build one management team, with the stores as the central focus. Interestingly, he also stated that there would be two experimental new store formats up and running within six months. These stores became "risk-free zones" where new ideas could be tried, and those that worked transferred to the rest of the chain. Norman described the experimental stores as "points of light" that everyone could look to, to see the future. Even before his short-term survival moves had shown positive results, Norman was working to build the future.

Crisis Change Conditions   In crisis change the business faces clear-cut external and internal challenges. In these conditions, people inside and outside your organization will usually be aware of the situation and will be expecting—even demanding—that changes be made to save the business. There may be some exceptions, but these people can be usually be made to see the necessity for action quickly with the all-too-abundant and undeniable evidence of difficulty. The really tough issues are to come up with immediate actions that will stay the crisis and set the stage for subsequent recovery.

Management Issues   There is a typical set of issues that you will have to tackle in undertaking crisis change. Financial issues are usually a high priority, and the challenge will be to buy time. In a freestanding business, you have to convince bankers, suppliers, and perhaps customers to give you the benefit of the doubt and postpone any precipitate action that would put you out of business. If the crisis is in a business unit in a large company, the challenge is to convince senior managers to give you the time and money you need for a turnaround. In either case, you need to demonstrate that you understand the gravity of the situation. Archie Norman did so by immediately terminating Asda's CFO, and by instituting a pay freeze for all 71 000 employees, cutting off investment in new stores, and putting undeveloped store sites and a peripheral business up for sale—all within a period of one month. Asda's bankers recognized that Norman understood the financial difficulties facing the business, was taking appropriate action, and gave him their support.

An added difficulty in trying to manage your way out of crisis is that you are usually saddled with seriously depleted resources. As businesses slide through reactive conditions and into crisis, good people leave, assets are run into the ground, and external reputations are strained. There is a very real risk that this process may have gone beyond the point of no return.

You may also have to confront your own involvement in the business through the period of decline and fall. If you have been part of that period you will clearly have to break your links with the past—in your own thinking and actions and in the perception of others. The evidence suggests that outsiders may have the best chance of breaking the existing thinking, habits, and relationships that have led to the decline of businesses. Certainly the decision to appoint Lou Gerstner, who knew nothing of the computer business, to take the helm of a rapidly declining IBM, must have seemed like a major gamble. But he dramatically reversed the company's fortunes—a task which a succession of IBM insiders had been unable to do. Crisis situations usually require fresh leadership.

If you are a new arrival, like Lou Gerstner or Archie Norman, you have probably inherited the management team that created the crisis. These may not be the best people to figure out how to save the business and work through the tough conditions of a turnaround. But one of the realities of crisis change is that you may be stuck with these managers, whether you like it or not; it is difficult to recruit new talent to a business that looks as if it is going down the drain. Archie Norman judged that he would be able to attract one or two senior outsiders to Asda, but for the first year or two he thought that he was going to have to depend heavily on people who, in his words, "could not really do the job."

Anticipatory Change

The circumstances of anticipatory change are at quite the opposite end of the spectrum from the clarity and desperation of crisis. This, unfortunately, is a mixed blessing. Anticipatory conditions allow you time to think and to act in a considered way; but the coincident lack of pressure or perceived urgency can pose a formidable obstacle to change. Consider the case of Pepsi's North American soft drink operations in the late 1980s and early 1990s.[3]

The 1980s were a very successful period for this Pepsi business, as earnings growth regularly topped 15 percent per year. Pepsi North America, with its "Pepsi Challenge" advertising campaign claiming that consumers preferred the taste of Pepsi to Coke, was widely viewed as a more entrepreneurial organization than Coca-Cola. In 1990, growth and profitability were still strong, and the outlook for the new decade was for more of the same.

But Craig Weatherup, who had taken over as Pepsi's North American president in 1987, was worried by a number of factors, both inside and outside the company, even though they had not yet impinged on the business. His primary concerns were that the rate of growth of soft drinks, especially colas, was slowing, and private-label cola sales were starting to increase. In addition, Pepsi was not able to increase prices due to fierce rivalry with Coke, and Coke was widening its lead in terms of volume of cola sold, because of its extensive distribution though fountain sales in outlets like McDonald's.

By mid 1990 Weatherup definitely felt that "things weren't right," and he spent some months interviewing industry experts, customers, and employees to develop a better feel for the situation. In September he met with his 10 direct reports to try and convince them of the urgency that he now felt for change. As he later stated, Weatherup was trying to get his managers to see overnight the unpalatable vision of the future that he had taken months to develop for himself. He painted a stark choice for his team. They could continue as they were and be a mediocre bottling company with a 5 to 10 percent annual growth rate, or they could strive for an annual target of 15 percent growth per year and be one of the premier companies in the United States.

Setting aside whatever misgivings they had (and Weatherup did admit there were areas of doubt in the external picture that he had painted for his team), Pepsi's senior managers began thinking about how to bring change to an organization that was performing well, and saw no particular need to change. An initial brainstorming session of the 10 managers produced a list of 35 potential "change levers," ranging from buying franchises to an increased focus on the customer, and they voted as to which would be the best place to start.

As might be expected, the change process was not as orderly and linear as first envisaged. Many employees did not see the need for change, and senior management did not want to push too far until everyone was on board. As a result, the journey took several years and led Pepsi North America into the creation of a vision statement; a major process re-engineering effort; the creation of a "total beverage" strategy, which took the company into iced tea, juice, and "new age" drinks; and finally to a reorganization which broke the business into 107 profit centres, where there had previously been one.

By 1993, Weatherup's persistence was paying off. Operating profit from Pepsi's domestic soft drink operations was growing at more than 15 percent per year, and the operating margin was approximately 16 percent, up from 12.5 percent in 1989. With hindsight one could argue that Weatherup's ability to manage "ahead of the curve" saved his business from an almost certain downturn in performance in the mid 1990s.

Anticipatory Change Conditions   In anticipatory change situations, strategic performance is healthy. A look out of the window at today's environment would reinforce today's strategy. The events of concern are events of the future; they have yet to have any impact on the business. And whatever the opportunities or problems that lie ahead, they are uncertain in their precise nature, their intensity, and their potential impact on the business.

Management Issues   The strategic issues that you face in tackling an anticipatory change situation are the result of the uncertainties facing the business. The problem that you are dealing with is simply not that clear. Under these circumstances it is essential to figure out how you can balance the risks of omission and commission: to do nothing puts the business at risk of being late or unable to deal with the forecast developments. To go too far, however, might commit the business to strategic changes that turn out to be dead wrong. Did Pepsi need to change? How much? How fast? Was re-engineering an appropriate response to the issues the business faced? Was the total beverage strategy the right move— or should the company have put all its energy into its core cola products? All of these issues were hotly debated.

A second issue in managing anticipatory change is the lack of a sense of urgency for change among the people in the organization. The business has been doing well, after all, and most employees have been doing pretty well, too. It is one of the frustrations of anticipatory situations that you may be the only one who is convinced there is a need for change. And, given the actual uncertainties of the situation, you have a limited ability to prove that change is necessary.

A third management issue in anticipatory change involves your personal credibility. The problems of managing in an ill-defined situation with minimal perceived urgency put a premium on credibility. To be effective in anticipatory change you need to have, or to build, and preserve credibility. It may be your prime resource as you try to marshal action in anticipation of the long-term challenges. In this respect, Craig Weatherup was well placed. He had led this Pepsi business during some very successful years, and was both well liked and well respected. A manager new to the business would probably have had a far more difficult task in persuading the organization that difficult times lay ahead. The reality for all managers is that the ambiguity of anticipatory situations means your credibility will always be tested. If you don't seem to have done your homework, or if you are wrong too often, you will lose the capacity to influence the direction of the business.

Reactive Change

The conditions of reactive change fall between those of anticipatory and crisis change. Strategic performance has gone over the top and is sliding. The nature of the challenge facing the business is becoming increasingly clear. Consider the case of a major player in the global aluminum business: Pechiney of France.

In the late 1980s Pechiney was performing very well. Its aluminum business was strong, and aluminum prices were high. In 1988 the company diversified into the packaging business, with the acquisition of American National Can of Chicago (the world's largest producer of Coke cans). Shortly thereafter, performance begin to slide. As aluminum prices fell, Pechiney's relatively high costs become increasingly evident, and in addition, all was not well in the newly acquired American business. By 1992 the company was doing little better than breaking even, and a moderate loss was posted in 1993. Performance was still sliding and debt levels rising when Jean-Pierre Rodier was brought into the company as Chairman and CEO in 1994.

Although Pechiney was not in crisis, Rodier concluded that if major change initiatives were not begun immediately, it soon would be. Adding to his sense of urgency was the fact that the French government, which owned the company, wanted to privatize it, but in mid 1994 it was in no shape to be offered to shareholders, other than at fire-sale prices. Rodier concluded that Pechiney needed focus and it needed to reduce its debt. Both objectives could be accomplished by selling businesses that were non-core, and after a quick but thorough analysis a number of businesses were sold in 1995. But selling businesses does not improve the operating results of the remaining businesses, and once these sales, and the privatization, were accomplished, Rodier concluded that bringing about significant and sustainable ongoing improvement in the now reduced Pechiney portfolio of businesses was his major challenge.

In early 1996 Rodier implemented what was known as the Pechiney Challenge Program. This program was designed to ensure that every business within the group would reach, by the end of 1998, profitability levels equivalent to those of their best competitors. Primarily focused on cost reduction, the overall targets were set by Rodier and his most senior managers, but determining exactly where and how the cuts would be made was up to the management teams in the various business units.

Shortly after Rodier announced the Challenge Program inside the company, he also made a public announcement of the Challenge targets. This meant that his personal credibility was now very much at stake. The Chairman had made a commitment to the shareholders that this program would succeed, and no one could doubt that his full energy would be behind it. Any manager who did not deliver would be letting down the Chairman in a very visible way.

By the end of 1997 the program was on target. The direct cost base had been reduced by approximately 10 percent, and the company had returned to profitability, although there was still substantial progress to be made. During that year a second program, Challenge Revenue, was launched, which had as its objective increasing revenue and profitability by improving the company's competitive advantage in its various businesses, and maximizing margins through adjustments of the product mix. Once again, the details of how this would be done were up to the individual businesses.

Reactive Change Conditions   In reactive change situations strategic performance is sliding, the nature of the external changes is becoming evident, and the impact of these changes on the business is building. If you were to forecast performance at this time, assuming no adjustments by the business, you would project the business into crisis. The period of time before the situation becomes critical is your *time to crisis*. It establishes a tangible measure of urgency for action and quite obviously puts the ultimate time horizon on your work.

Management Issues   A common strategic issue in reactive change is that of concentrating attention on the core business and developing an effective strategic response to the changing conditions. There may be a tremendous range of ideas in management about how to respond to the now recognizable challenges to the business. This was the situation in Pechiney. But what the business needs is a focused and effective counterattack in its key markets. Competitors are taking the lead and time is passing—it will take a concentrated effort to catch up and regain a secure position. Pechiney's costs were far above those of major competitors like Alcan and Alcoa. Managers needed to be persuaded that strategic proposals that may make sense under other conditions, such as acquisitions or alliances, may only detract from the attention required by the core business.

The need for focus, the pressure of time, and the possibility of resistance mean that the power to press for change is important in reactive circumstances. You need power to make things happen. Jean-Pierre Rodier, selected by the French government to run the company, had such power, but translating that into tangible action throughout the company is nevertheless a formidable challenge, particularly when one is new to the industry and the company.

ORGANIZATIONAL READINESS FOR CHANGE

Organizational readiness is the second critical variable defining the starting conditions for a change plan. Readiness refers to the commitment (or lack of it) that people feel to making the changes required by the situation the business faces, and their ability to perform the new tasks that will be required of them. To focus our assessment of readiness, we will work with *target groups* and *target group readiness*.

Target Group Identification

While most strategic changes will involve a wide range of people in a business, it is important to isolate the individuals and groups who will be particularly crucial at the start of the process. These might be senior managers whose support or resistance will most influence the success of the proposal. In Pepsi, for example, it was quite clear that Craig Weatherup would not get very far without the support of the most senior line people in the organization, and his first priority was to win them over to the 15 percent per year growth objective, and to convince them that this could not be achieved without significant change. In other situations the target groups might be plant managers, particular country organizations, or perhaps certain functional groups, who will have to be heavily involved in the change process.

As we will elaborate later, broad, unfocused change programs run into problems. By isolating a limited number of change targets—namely, the individuals and groups who are critical to the first steps of change—you can start to focus your assessment of readiness and increase the precision of your preliminary actions. This is a simple, practical necessity.

Target Group Readiness

It is useful to work with two stages of readiness in assessing how prepared your target group is for change. The first of these stages is the *sense of commitment* in the target groups: do they agree that the changes being discussed are necessary and appropriate, and will they play an active role in developing and supporting the changes, or will they resist the steps that are being put forward? The second is *capability:* given that they feel the changes are appropriate, do the target groups have the skills needed to undertake the changes being discussed? Commitment and capability are discussed further below.

Target Group Commitment   A variety of factors will affect the commitment of your target groups to adopt and implement change. If they understand and accept the need for change, and feel that the proposed changes are appropriate and are not personally threatening, it is likely that they will collaborate and the changes will proceed with minimal difficulty. Unfortunately, change is seldom this tidy.

Lack of commitment to change can come from many sources. At the simplest level, your intended target groups may be unaware of the need for change. They may be deliberately or inadvertently isolated from the market and business performance data that indicate change is required. It is not too hard to imagine an engineering group at Pechiney, for example, with its head down, doing its job of sustaining the firm's world-leading smelting technology, somewhat oblivious to developments on the competitive front, and prepared to assume that because things were going well in its corner of the business, all is well.

Another concern is that individuals and groups may downplay or deny the urgency of a situation because they really don't want to face up to the realities. Some people in Asda, for example, may have seen signs that a crisis was developing before it arrived, but chose, consciously or not, to minimize its likelihood or impact because the alternative of responding to the signs may have seemed to be so disruptive and painful. Put several of these individuals together and you may end up with *groupthink,* in which members of the target group find common support for their perspective and add force to the denial of the need to change.

On the other hand, some people may see a need for change, but genuinely disagree with the direction that the change is taking. In the early months of

Rodier's change initiative at Pechiney, for example, there was natural resistance to the idea of selling what were in some cases extremely healthy businesses that had been in the Pechiney "family" for a number of years and had certainly done "nothing wrong." The 1995 sale of Howmet, a well-managed and profitable business in the United States, was a case in point. Similarly in Asda, the notion of selling land that was earmarked for future store expansion seemed to some like giving up on the future.

Others might resist because they think (perhaps rightly) they will end up losing position, power, compensation, prestige, perks, and so on. People see themselves as potential losers as changes are made and they dig in to defend their positions. The best that you can hope for here is that the opposition emerges as open resistance, because then you can assess it and determine how to proceed. There may be ways to negotiate or to get the resistors onside, or you may have to move them out of the way. The task will be difficult. You may not win, but at least you know what you are dealing with.

The toughest situation is that of deliberate passive resistance, of which the most destructive form is compliance on the surface while foot dragging underneath. Jack Welch ran into an abundance of this in his work to transform General Electric. As reported by Tichy and Sherman: "Some business chiefs stolidly thwarted Welch's plans . . . . Rather than oppose the CEO directly, they would say yes, when they meant no, doing what they thought best for their businesses instead of pushing Welch's agenda of change."[4] Managers possess an enormous power in their capacity to do nothing, or at least to do nothing that really contributes to the direction of change. Such deliberate passive resistance is very hard to identify and to pin down, except over a period of time. You have to be aware that it can happen, watch for it throughout a program of change, and bring it to the surface. The potential for passive resistance also carries a warning for managers who would impose change by force. There are many ways, particularly in the short term, that people can avoid doing what you want them to do. In this respect, the effective balance of power is on their side.

All of these forms of resistance feed on ambiguity and are thus more likely to be encountered in anticipatory and reactive change conditions than in crisis. The uncertainty in both the Pepsi and Pechiney situations, for example, suggested that resistance would be a factor to contend with. The force of events in crisis, however, such as in Asda, helped to coalesce people around survival and to generate a willingness to get on with whatever needed to be done.

From an analytic standpoint every potential key player in the change process needs to be assessed in terms of his or her commitment to change. Where there are problems, the diagnosis has to go deeper, to identify the source of the resistance and the power of that person or group to frustrate the change program. We will discuss this process further in the next chapter.

Target Group Capability　In the Diamond-E analysis of your business you will have considered the broad capabilities of management and its support people and incorporated this assessment into your strategic decisions. The current analysis is different in two ways. First, it brings the focus down to the specific individuals and groups that are critical to your intentions for change. Are these potential target groups able to understand the situation and respond creatively and effectively to it? Do the plant managers at Pechiney have the skills, for example, to deliver the cost reductions that they have promised? Do store managers at Asda have the skills required for a radical program of store renewal?

Second, your options for dealing with gaps between the available and required skills in your target groups narrow as you move from anticipatory to crisis change. In anticipatory change there is time for training and development and for the evolution of strategic responses to the external change. As the business moves towards crisis, however, there is less time for the development of new skills. In crisis you pretty well have to work with what you have—there is no time for training, and the possibilities of recruiting people with the required skills are limited by the crisis conditions. As we stated earlier, Archie Norman had to work with the management he had on hand at Asda and with the skills that they already possessed. This is one of the reasons why in crisis it is so common to shrink and focus the business—you are trying to simplify the business to the point where it can be run successfully by the existing talent.

At first glance the issue of capability is cut and dried. You know what skills you need, and you will try to devise ways to acquire or develop them in the time available. There is a second-order effect, however, that you should look out for: if managers don't possess the skills that they think they will need to run the business in a different way, they have all the more reason to deny the problem, or to resist attempts to deal with it until it is in crisis. To this end, training does more than provide a new skill set. It provides people with the confidence that they will survive if they tackle the realities of the business, and an understanding that this is better done sooner than later.

PERSONAL READINESS FOR CHANGE

The third factor to be assessed in setting up the starting conditions for change is your own involvement in the situation. In an ideal world you would have the knowledge, power, and will to implement whatever changes come on the agenda. In reality, however, your strengths and weaknesses in relation to the change problem and targets are an inseparable part of the change conditions and should be an important influence on your choice of an action plan. These strengths and weaknesses define your personal readiness to lead the change process.

We will discuss personal readiness in terms of commitment and capability, just as we did in the organizational readiness section, with the major difference being that you have to work with these issues from two perspectives: your own and that of the prime target individuals and groups. Jean-Pierre Rodier at Pechiney may be confident that he sufficiently understands the aluminum and packaging industries, for example, but the veterans in the company may think quite differently. You have to assess your readiness from both a personal and external perspective.

Personal Commitment   This may seem like a curious item to raise since you are already positioned in the role of a change agent. But it is important that you assess your commitment to see the change through and pay the price that this requires. Changes don't come easily and it is well worth thinking about whether this is something you really want to do. This is more than a matter of personal preference. Others will sense your conviction, and test your commitment, and if they aren't convinced then you and the change program will be in trouble. If Weatherup had decided to lead the change at Pepsi even though he wasn't really convinced that the changes were necessary and that the admittedly high costs were worthwhile, then there would have been real problems down the road. It is better to think this question through in advance to prepare yourself, and, if you are not sufficiently committed, to see what can be done to bring in others to deal with the situation.

As you assess your commitment for change, you should consider the related issue of the urgency with which the change is required. It is important to distinguish between the urgency that you feel—which will be a major factor underlying your commitment—and the urgency that actually attaches to the business situation. Aggressive managers may feel greater urgency than the business problem dictates, because of their personalities, perhaps, or their interpretation of their assignments. They want action now, but the business case is actually not that pressing. This is not necessarily a problem because, given a choice, it is better to press for earlier and faster change than later and slower change. But if urgency driven by personal motives is not carefully considered it can lead to premature and inappropriate actions.

As well, your personal desire to act quickly can give rise to resistance. If others think you are on a personal rather than a business agenda, the whole process of change might be stalled or become unnecessarily contentious. A reasonable example of this occurs in the foreign affiliates of many multinational companies. Local management becomes accustomed to new presidents and other senior officers being moved in and out by the parent. They also understand that these executives want to come in and change things quickly to make their mark before they move on to new assignments. The acid test that the locals will put to these rotating executives is simple: are they dealing with real business needs or their own career needs? The degree of local cooperation or, conversely, the degree of local resistance will vary accordingly.

The key point here is to be aware of the possibility of a difference between your personal urgency and commitment to change and that required by the external conditions. This may mean that you have to speed up if you are behind. It certainly does not mean you have to slow down if you are ahead, but in this case you have to consider the issues of being out front and deal with them as part of your action plan.

Personal Capability   In considering your own ability to lead the change program, ask yourself whether you have the skills to understand the circumstances and to act effectively to deal with them. If there are gaps in your knowledge, one of your first tasks will be to close them—by some personal education but also by recruiting people internally or externally that will bring the needed skills to the situation.

The target groups in your change situation will interpret your capability in terms of credibility and power and you must do the same. In your own view and in that of others, are you a credible agent of change? In your own view and that of others, do you have the ability to manage people effectively, the power to make things happen and, if necessary, roll over opposition? The answers are obviously crucial to your approach and will affect the tactics that you can employ. In the Asda situation, for example, Archie Norman's previous experience at turning around Woolworth's, another struggling U.K. retailer, was well known to the management team he inherited at Asda, and was an important factor underlying his ability to move as quickly as he did.

SUMMARY

This chapter is the first of two dealing with the move from broad strategic prescriptions for change to the specific and detailed actions to put those changes into place. We presented a process for planning change that consists of four sequential steps: (1) identifying your change agenda; (2) identifying starting conditions; (3) developing guidelines for change; and (4) creating a specific action plan.

The chapter began with the recommendation that you create a change agenda, listing the broad changes that you identified in your Diamond-E analysis as necessary to support the strategy that you want to implement, paying particular attention to those that will require behavioural change.

Then we turned to starting conditions, which were discussed in terms of three considerations: the urgency for action, organizational readiness, and personal readiness. Urgency for action refers to the pressure to implement the strategic changes that you have in mind. Degrees of urgency are related to the strategic performance of the business and can vary from the immediacy of crisis situations to the low pressure and ambiguity of anticipatory change conditions. Organizational readiness depends on the commitment and capability of the individuals and groups who will be most instrumental to the change process. Personal readiness refers to the commitment and capability that you bring to the situation as the manager who is going to lead the change process.

The change agenda and starting conditions for every change project will be unique. There is no standard recipe that will lead to success in all change situations. You need to understand your particular change agenda and starting conditions well, before you begin to establish guidelines for action and an action plan. These are the topics to which we turn in Chapter 10.

NOTES

1. A list of "eight steps to transforming your organization" is contained in John Kotter's article "Leading Change: Why Transformation Efforts Fail," *Harvard Business Review* (March–April 1995). This is a good example of a generic approach to change. The steps are useful, but in any given situation some will be critical; others unimportant.

2. The Asda story is taken from James Weber and Michael Beer, Asda (A), (A-1), (B), (C), cases 498-005–498-008. Boston, Mass.: Harvard Business School, 1998.

3. The Pepsi story is taken from Don Sull and David A. Garvin, Pepsi's Regeneration, 1990–1993, case 395-048. Boston: Harvard Business School, 1994.

4. Noel M. Tichy and Stafford Sherman, *Control Your Destiny or Someone Else Will* (New York: Doubleday, 1993), p. 84.

ADDITIONAL READINGS

BEER, MICHAEL, RUSSEL A. EISENSTAT, AND BERT SPECTOR, "Why Change Programs Don't Produce Change," *Harvard Business Review* (November–December 1990), p. 158.

GHOSHAL, SUMANTRA AND CHRISTOPHER A. BARTLETT, "Rebuilding Behavioural Context: A Blueprint for Corporate Renewal," *Sloan Management Review* (Winter 1996), p. 23.

JON R. KATZENBACH, *Real Change Leaders*. London: Nicholas Brealey, 1996.

RICHARD PASCALE, MARK MILLEMANN AND LINDA GIOJA, "Changing the Way We Change," *Harvard Business Review* (November–December 1997), p. 127.

STRATEGIC CHANGE: GUIDELINES AND ACTION

In this chapter we assume that you have worked through the material in Chapter 9, identifying your change agenda and starting conditions, and are ready to translate these into guidelines for action and a detailed plan for change.

ESTABLISHING GUIDELINES FOR ACTION

In Figure 9.1 we proposed that you establish four guidelines for action: (1) priority objectives, which are those things that you want to accomplish first; (2) priority actions, which indicate your priority targets and the first action steps you will take with each; (3) leadership style, which establishes how you are going to manage the change process; and (4) pace, which determines how rapidly you should proceed. We will discuss these in order.

PRIORITY OBJECTIVES

At the outset of your change program you established a change agenda which resulted from your Diamond-E analysis. The items on your agenda included things like changing your organization structure or management processes to create behavioural change, hiring people with new skills, acquiring a new technology, stopping the negative cash flow in a crisis, and so on. We suggested that you pay particular attention to those items that were likely to require new behaviour, because these are all too often overlooked or underestimated.

Now, having assessed the urgency of your change situation and the readiness of key groups and individuals in your organization for change, you are ready to determine your most pressing objectives. Which of the items on your change agenda should you address first? How many items should you try to deal with at the same time? Should you focus intensely on a few objectives, or take a much broader approach?

Behavioural Versus Non-Behavioural Objectives

When preparing your change agenda you differentiated between items that were designed to produce behavioural change and those that were not. We continue that distinction here. Your priority objectives list will include items of each type, and you need to think carefully about how to blend the two. Some managers, for example, instinctively tend to shun the behaviour-related issues, preferring instead to focus on "easier to manage" issues like making an acquisition, or selling a business. If you find yourself focusing exclusively on items that do not lead to behaviour change, beware—you may be kidding yourself about what your true priorities should be.

For an example let us return to the situation facing Tom Stephens at MacMillan Bloedel ("MacBlo") referred to in Chapter 1. For many years, MacBlo had had the best inventory of trees on the west coast of Canada, but its logging costs were the highest in the world, due in part to the adversarial relationship between the company and its unions. Rather than try to reduce costs by changing the behaviour of its managers or of the unions, previous senior MacBlo managers had chosen to diversify the company's efforts into other product lines, and other areas of the world. Stephens' approach was different. He decided that he would focus on the core West Coast business and work to change the traditional patterns of management and union behaviour.[1]

Stephens judged that without hitting the behavioural issues head-on, he would not make any real progress, and he decided to pursue simultaneously two sets of objectives: one involving portfolio changes, to be achieved by selling parts of the business, and the other to effect behavioural changes in the core business. Whether he will be successful remains to be seen, but he gets full marks for not making the common mistake of setting his objectives only in terms of substantive changes and underestimating the importance of changes required in behaviour.

Our primary focus in this chapter is on the challenge of bringing about behavioural change in an organization. That is not to say that other changes are unimportant. In fact, you may want to make a significant substantive change— sell a business, raise new equity, or make an acquisition, for example—to demonstrate that you are serious about change. But generally it is the behavioural changes that are the most problematic, and that is where we will concentrate.

ACTION PRIORITIES

As you set about determining how to achieve your key objectives, you must address two key questions: (1) whose behaviour do you want to change, and (2) how are you going to change it? The answers to these two questions make up your action priorities.

Priority Targets

In your analysis of starting conditions you identified the individuals and groups that will be most involved in or affected by the anticipated changes and assessed their commitment and capability for change. All of these people will sooner or later be involved in the change process, but the immediate question is with whom should you start; these people will be your priority targets.

An important first step in determining who will be priority targets is to assess each potential target in terms of his or her commitment to the proposed changes, and the capabilities that they could bring to the change program. Do not try to make this assessment for everyone in the company, however. If you judge, for example, that your plant management personnel are going to be critical to the success of your change program, focus on them, and decide who among them should become priority targets. To do this, take the plant managers and sort them into groups as indicated in Figure 10.1. The groups are described as follows:

Change Agents are people who believe that change is necessary, and that the proposed changes make sense. Furthermore, they have the skills and capability to help bring about the change. In short, they are competent and committed managers who are your potential allies in the change process. In most change situations, there are fewer individuals in this category than the others. In anticipatory situations it will be the commitment that is missing; in crisis competence may be lacking.

Change Agents in Waiting are those who would like the change program to be successful, but do not have the skills to be of much help. Given time and training, they might develop such skills, and whether you decide that these individuals should be priority targets will depend in part on how much time you believe you have to implement the change program.

FIGURE 10.1

Assessing
Potential
Priority Targets

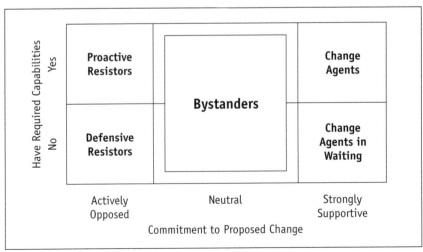

Bystanders would prefer to wait and see how the change process fares before making a commitment to it. They may not have the energy needed to get involved, they may prefer to avoid the perceived risk of involvement, or they may be skeptical of "yet another initiative." Whatever the cause, turning a bystander into a change agent will take some convincing, and possibly some training.

163

Defensive Resistors are opposed to the change initiative, probably because they realize that they do not have the capabilities to play a meaningful role in it, and thus find the change program threatening. If the change program is successful, they could lose out. If these individuals are likely to be disruptive you may have to deal with them early in the process; more often, they do not receive attention until later.

Proactive Resistors are competent managers who think that your change initiative is inappropriate. They either believe that change is not required, or that the particular changes you are proposing are not the right ones. These people could be worth listening to, because they may be right. We know of one senior manager who spent time with such resistors early in his ("reactive") change process, rather than working with change agents (which would have been much more comfortable) because he thought he might have something to learn from them. In addition, he believed that if he could convert one or two of them into change agents (there were five active resistors) the others would feel isolated, and as an extra benefit, this visible change of commitment by active resistors might generate new commitment to the change process on the part of some bystanders. As it turned out, this approach was successful.

To decide which of these potential targets should get your early attention, you need to integrate the other starting conditions into your analysis—particularly the urgency for action and your power position relative to the potential targets. If you are dealing with anticipatory change, for example, there is little value in targeting resistors at the outset, since the case for change will be too ambiguous. Better to seek and to develop change agents and build momentum to influence the resistors. If you are in reactive change, however, you may have no option but to target and take on resistors and bystanders who are in a position to block progress. Here it is important to understand your powers relative to these targets and how they can be best employed in the limited time available.

In fact, you may not discover any attractive priority targets—people who can and will do what needs to be done in the time available. Schindler Elevators of Switzerland faced such a situation after it purchased the Westinghouse elevator and escalator businesses in 1989. The escalator business was performing poorly, and part of the problem was that it had been sourcing poor quality escalators from a Korean joint venture. One logical way forward would have been to move escalator manufacturing into an underutilized former Westinghouse elevator plant. But employees in this heavily unionized, high-cost facility in the U.S. Northeast were judged to be lacking both the capabilities and the attitudes needed to support the changes that would be required to produce escalators efficiently. The decision was made, not to try and drive change in that plant, but to construct a new plant in the South, transferring former Westinghouse managers who seemed ready to try a new way of doing business, and hiring a new workforce. A huge amount of energy was focused on that plant, and both management and newly hired unskilled workers became the priority change targets.

Picking Starting Points for Action

Once you have chosen your priority targets, you need to decide what action you are going to take *vis-à-vis* each. There are two competing theories about this. The conventional approach is determined by *commitment and capability:* you start by preparing your priority targets for change by creating a sense of urgency, developing skills and commitment to the required changes, and then move logically through the structural or process changes designed to change behaviour. This is obviously a reasonable progression, but it can get bogged down in well-intended, but diffuse and ineffective action that has little ultimate impact on results. Schaffer and Thompson, for example, criticize the pursuit of this sequence as a "raindance" of activities that sound good, look good, and allow managers to feel good, but which have little impact on the bottom line. They cite as an example a three-year change program in a mineral extraction company that had accomplished 50 percent of its training goals, 50 percent of its employee participation goals, but only 5 percent of its results goals.[2]

In contrast to readiness-driven change is *results*-driven change, in which a set of precise and measurable results are specified, and people are made responsible for producing them. The results-driven approach does not ignore the obvious need for other organizational and readiness changes, but it develops them as necessary in a process that works primarily to support results. This approach keeps attention focused on the bottom line, but by forcing change and higher performance standards on people who are not ready for it, the whole endeavour may blow up in your face. Change is seldom risk-free!

In the end, you will tailor your starting points for action to the target in question, and to the starting conditions that you are working from. Thus, if you are in anticipatory change, like Craig Weatherup of Pepsi (Chapter 9), you have little option but to start with actions to improve readiness; if you are in crisis change, like Archie Norman at Asda (also Chapter 9), you are going to have to specify and achieve some immediate behaviour changes that will produce new capabilities and improved results.

As you work through your selection of priority targets and your intended starting points for each, collect your thoughts in a chart such as that shown in

Table 10.1. As you do this, you should be asking yourself if you have focused too widely, or perhaps too narrowly. Do you have the balance right between focus and scope?

Focus Versus Scope

How much should you try to do at once? In a crisis, the answer is probably "a lot."[3] But in anything short of a crisis situation you will need to make some fine judgments about how widely to diffuse your time and energy. Singling out a small number of priority targets, for example, will permit you to focus your effort, but postpones work with people who will ultimately be important to the total program. Starting out with multiple targets, on the other hand, gives you the comfort of covering all the bases, but disperses your impact and may mean that your program will stall. Much will depend on the commitment for change across the potential targets, your own power, and the urgency of the situation. A high degree of readiness will allow you to work successfully with more people, whereas significant pockets of resistance will call for a more focused approach.

Avoid the temptation to take on too much at once. Evidence from studies of simultaneous multi-target, multi-objective change programs shows that they just don't work well—there is too much to manage and there are too many opportunities for slippage.[4] In the Schindler example just cited, the decision to focus energy on a single manufacturing facility proved to be a good one, as this plant became the low-cost producer in the industry and was selected by Industry Week magazine as one of the "ten best plants in the USA" in 1995. Schindler then

TABLE 10.1
Priority Targets and Starting Points

Priority Targets	Starting Points for Action				
	Improve Readiness for Behaviour Change		Drive Behaviour Change		
	Increase Capability	Increase Commitment	Change Organization Structure	Change Your Management Processes	Change Ways of Managing People
Target Group 1					
Target Group 2					
Target Group 3					

created rivalry between the new plant and others in the United States and Europe to drive change throughout the company.

Focusing change efforts often seems like a sacrifice at the beginning of a change program, because of the things that you are *not* doing, like improving the existing plants, but it is often a better way to begin. If you feel that you must deal with many targets at the same time, you might try focusing them intensely on a single item from your change agenda which will give a direction and energy for change and then, when that has run its course, to pick another item to re-focus and reenergize the corporation. This was done by Jean-Pierre Rodier of Pechiney (Chapter 9), who, after focusing on getting the company's portfolio of businesses right in 1994 and 1995, created behaviour and attitude changes across a large number of managers via a two-year cost-reduction effort, and then in 1997 unveiled a new program focusing on revenue enhancement. Each of these "waves of change" created new energy across a broad group of managers.

LEADERSHIP STYLE

Your leadership style determines how you intend to relate to target individuals or groups and what specific tactics you will employ. We have described two very different styles in Table 10.2. Any particular approach that you choose will likely fall between these two extremes. The first style consists of a very *directive* approach to a target, with tactics that centre on instruction and pressure to create a change in behaviour. The second style is based on a *participative* approach to a target, with tactics that focus on guiding and facilitating changes in behaviour.

Some writers and consultants present one or the other of these styles as the single best way to achieve change. Our approach, however, is to focus on choosing the style that best suits the conditions that you are dealing with. Indeed, the question is seldom one of settling on a fixed style, but one of determining the right blend of styles.

Directive Leadership

There are a variety of simple terms to describe the directive style: autocratic, command, coercive, top-down, and so on. The crucial assumptions behind the style are that you understand the problems, know the solutions, and have the power to force compliance with your views. The tactical approach is straightforward, and involves (1) communicating the reasons for change to establish urgency; (2) defining the intended changes and telling people what to do (although targets might be given some participatory role in detailed execution); (3) training as necessary to perform the new tasks; (4) monitoring progress closely and adjusting instructions as necessary; and (5) implementing incentives and punishments to ensure that these tasks are executed and sustained.

TABLE 10.2
Key Features of Directive and Participative Leadership Styles

	Characteristics	Benefits	Risks
Directive	• Directive • Assumes initiator understands problem, knows solution, has power • Tactics focus on communication of reasons, instructions, expectations	• Fast • Efficient • Economizes on initiator time, energy	• Wrong diagnosis, wrong remedy • Passive or active resistance • Pseudo change • High after-the-fact costs
Participative	• Participative • Assumes that diagnosis and remedy will be developed in change process • Tactics focus on collaborative exploration of causes, development of remedies, building commitment	• Effective • Flexible • Develops and tests problem and people at same time	• Too slow • Potential to run off track • Avoidance of tough decisions

If you operate as an impersonal, cut-and-dried, mechanical leader, you will likely run into trouble. The directive style doesn't assume that you are, or that you should necessarily act, that way. There is room for variety in the approach to make it more acceptable to people you are dealing with. Charismatic leadership, for example, is for the most part directive leadership, with emotion and enthusiasm serving as the foundations for the leader's power.

The benefits of a directive approach to change are substantial. If it works, you achieve change quickly and with an economy of effort. However, the change program can easily get off track or fail. There isn't much room for correction as you go down this path. A perception that you are wrong, or on a power trip, or unable to sustain the pressure may encourage resistance. Or people may change their behaviour while you are around, and then revert to their old ways as soon as you move on. Finally, your relationship with the targets, and their willingness to work in the new situation and to contribute to the next change may all suffer. These risk possibilities may sound severe, but there *are* situations in which directive leadership is both desirable and attainable.

The Choice of a Directive Style   The most natural setting for a directive leadership style is in crisis-change situations, when the circumstances of the business demand fast action. The people in the business, by and large, are waiting for decisive leadership; in fact, they are likely calling for it. These conditions confer power on the leader. The definite theme of action will be directive— quick decisions, clear orders, and a minimal tolerance for reluctant execution.

A second natural setting for a directive approach is during a reactive change, when a standoff has developed between the proponents and opponents of change. In the meantime precious time is wasting. You have a mini-crisis situation on your hands. The sensible way to break the impasse is with a clear and focused application of power.

Finally, you would probably *not* want to use a directive approach in anticipatory change situations. On most of these occasions, if you are honest with yourself, you will admit that you simply don't know enough about the problems and the solutions to charge ahead into directed change. If you decide to do so anyway, the probability of minimal readiness and the possibilities for effective resistance will put you in a very difficult position. The possible exception is when you are trying to start a change process not because you see decay ahead, but simply because you feel that today's performance can be improved. In such a situation, you may be directive about the performance target, but participative when it comes to deciding how it might be achieved.

The Participative Style

There are a variety of simple terms to describe the participative style: bottom-up, collaborative, empowering, shared, and so on. The crucial assumptions behind the style are that an effective diagnosis and remedy can be developed in the course of the change process. The basic tactics of a participative approach are to (1) involve the target individuals and groups in studies of the situation to help clarify the reasons for change and to establish urgency; (2) collaborate, debate, and negotiate with these people to define the needed changes and the detailed steps of change; (3) train as necessary to perform the new tasks; (4) delegate significant responsibility for monitoring and adjusting implementation; and (5) install incentives and punishments to support the continuing execution of the new tasks.

The participative style is not a dereliction of duty. Rather, it requires you to think carefully through the steps of working with the targets and to exercise the patience and the determination needed to see that process through. There will definitely be junctures at which you will have to take control, and use directive tactics. A crucial skill is sensing when this needs to be done and how far you can go without poisoning the whole process. What you can expect is that it will be very hard work and make major demands on your time.

The merits of the participative approach are substantial. If it works as intended it produces effective solutions by employing the analytic and creative faculties of the people closest to the problems, and it harnesses the energy of those same people to implement and make the solutions work. However, there are substantial risks as well. Participative change is slow—at least compared with directive change. Furthermore, a participative approach is vulnerable to producing compromise solutions that the targets want (or perhaps just the compromises that they can agree upon) rather than the tough measures that the business needs. Finally, there is a chance that the sheer momentum built by the process will get out of hand and challenge the leaders to commit to directions that they are still quite uneasy about.

The Choice of a Participative Style   The natural conditions for implementing the participative style are virtually the flip side of the conditions that favour the directive style. The most obviously appropriate conditions for using a participatory style are anticipatory change conditions, with their inherent need for better problem definition. There simply isn't enough time in crisis change for participative measures. The conditions of reactive change may require a mix of styles: participative to mobilize those who want to get on with the job, and directive to deal with the targets that hesitate too long, resist, or otherwise create bottlenecks in the process.

PACE

Pace is a term to describe the amount of change that you want to accomplish in a given period of time. It encompasses both the scope and the significance of the individual changes. A fast pace, for example, would be the pursuit of significant behavioural changes (perhaps new ways of handling specific issues) across a range of targets in a short period of time. A slow pace, in contrast, would be the pursuit of modest behavioural change (perhaps the recognition of some urgency for change) on the part of a few targets in the same time period.

Your decision about the pace of change has an important impact on your selection of action priorities and leadership style. A decision to try to work at a fast pace, for example, suggests aggressive objectives, a range of targets, and a directive style. The choice of a slower pace creates an opportunity to select less ambitious objectives, fewer targets, and a participative approach. Given its influence on the other change guidelines, pace should logically be the first of the guidelines that you settle on. We have dealt with it late in our order of presentation only because it is easier to understand its role after you appreciate the nature of the action priorities and leadership style guidelines.

There are two key factors to consider in setting the pace of change: (1) the urgency in the business situation, and (2) the urgency that you feel personally to press forward with the change. If the business urgency is high, as it is in crisis conditions, there is no room for personal choice—a fast pace is essential. But in anticipatory and reactive situations, business urgency only sets a minimum pace; there is room to move faster if you want to and if it makes sense. The time-to-crisis calculation in reactive change, for example, sets the time frame in which change must be accomplished, but it doesn't mandate that the process should take that long.

The decision to set a faster pace than business urgency dictates is a sensitive matter, as we discussed in Chapter 9. There are definite advantages in getting on with it, and moving to the next challenge. But if the haste of your personal agenda is likely to generate questionable decisions, or magnified resistance, the wise choice would be to slow down.

Implementing Pace Decisions

The best way to pin down the pace of your change plan is to think in terms of relatively short time periods, from perhaps a few days in a crisis situation to a maximum of 90 days in reactive and anticipatory change. By specifying how much you want to accomplish in, say, the first 90-day period, the second 90-day period, and so on, you build a plan that reaches from your starting point to your ultimate objectives.

A further advantage to specific, short time periods is that they allow you to break down a complex set of change requirements into workable projects based on what you intend to achieve and how you intend to achieve it. This helps you to move from general objectives to the specific practical actions required to achieve them.

By far the most critical time period is the first period. The decisions that you make about pace, action priorities, and tactics for this period set the tone for your total program. Perhaps the most telling question that anyone can ask about a plan for change is: What are you going to do in, say, the first 90 days? The answers will reveal much more about where the change plan is going, whether it has been thought through, and its likelihood of success, than some lofty generalities about longer term aims.

GENERIC GUIDELINES

In this section we will work through some guidelines for first steps in crisis, anticipatory, and reactive change to illustrate how to convert starting conditions into change guidelines and ultimately into detailed steps of change. These guidelines would be generally applicable in the early periods of change, and are summarized in Table 10.3. The normal caution is in order here: these guidelines aren't fixed rules or even universally applicable. They simply represent thought starters for your consideration in planning specific actions in specific situations.

Crisis Change

Crisis change demands urgent action; as Table 10.3 indicates, the pace of change will likely be a sprint. Further, while it is important to keep your actions simple and focused, multiple targets and multiple objectives will probably be necessary. Your tactical approach will also be mixed, encompassing a participative style with external targets and a directive style internally.

Preliminary Work   The first item on a crisis agenda, curiously, is to look forward and visualize (at least roughly) the nature, strategy, and viability of the business to be salvaged. This objective serves three purposes. First, it helps answer the question of whether the business is worth the cost and risk of the rescue attempt. Second, by outlining the shape of the future business, it helps identify what needs to be saved and what is expendable. Third, it is helpful in obtaining the external support necessary to weather the crisis.

There are two common errors made at this point in crisis situations. The first error is one of simply not planning, of reacting in an aimless way to the immediate pressures. Fate quickly intervenes to correct this error, often at the expense of the business's existence. The second fault lies in trying to save too much. This latter error is understandable since most managers would like to preserve as much as possible of the business. Surgical cuts in personnel, product lines, and so forth are distasteful. But attempting to preserve too much will complicate an already hazardous venture and substantially raise the risk of failure.

External Targets   Your negotiating position with external targets will usually boil down to balancing the costs for them of your going out of business with the

TABLE 10.3
Generic Change Guidelines

	Anticipatory Change	Reactive Change	Crisis Change	
Targets	• Supporters	• Pivotal Groups	• External	• Internal
First Steps	• Develop support and direction	• Organizational changes	• Buy time	• Make Strategic Changes
Style	• Participative	• Mixture	• Participative	• Directive
Timing	• Jog	• Run	• Sprint	• Sprint

benefits for them of your staying in business. If there is at least a reasonable case to be made for their support, then you can turn your attention to earning it. They may not exactly be willing partners, but like it or not, that is what they are, and you should set your tactics with them accordingly.

Securing support will require extensive face-to-face contact and a plan that passes muster under a critical eye. A probable condition for support by banks and other creditors will be plans and actions that reduce their exposure. Your recovery plan should anticipate this by liquidating redundant assets and pushing for operating efficiencies that will increase cash availability. As mentioned earlier, Archie Norman put land that had been earmarked for Asda's future expansion up for sale. He also replaced his Chief Financial Officer as part of his effort to regain credibility with the company's bankers.[5]

The support that you do obtain will likely be given on a very short-term basis, so an essential part of your plan must be to keep in contact with the key external parties over time, apprising them of progress and explaining your next steps. This task will be made more difficult by the usual pattern of performance in crisis, in which results almost inevitably get worse before they get better!

Internal Targets   Within the firm, your plan for crisis must quickly focus on two action priorities: the strategic changes that are required to simplify and downsize your business and the identification of the people that you want to stay with the business to implement them. These strategic decisions are necessary to meet financial requirements and to minimize the demands on existing management and processes. They will usually involve cutbacks in product lines, market involvements, facilities and so on, and will drive your handling of internal change targets.

First, decide who will stay and who will go, and act on your decision as soon as possible. Archie Norman dismissed his CFO on day one. As you will have minimal time and credibility to recruit new talent, the people whom you select to keep will be pretty much what you have to work with. This reinforces the need to make strategic changes that simplify the demands made on management, and it sets up the tactics for dealing with the people selected to carry through with the turnaround.

The circumstances of crisis change call for a straightforward application of directive tactics inside the business. The strategic decisions and the personnel cuts have to be implemented quickly, and you will be directly involved in communicating needs, handling decisions, supporting managers, and generally tying loose ends together. None of this will be simple, and speed is essential. You cannot possibly get every decision right, and you are unlikely to get consensus for every action. One of the managers at Asda made the following comment in 1996, looking back at the crisis the company had been through:

In any change effort, one third of the people are with you, one third are un-sure, but may come around, and one-third are not with you. Most of those not on board were rightly let go. Yet many of those who were unsure were also let go, never having been given the chance to change. Some of these people, I believe, were let go too quickly.[6]

After the Crisis Survival is your dominant goal at the time of crisis. Then, as the immediate threats are overcome, you need a period of time for stabilization. What is left of the business must be put on a solid footing. Changes should proceed at a slower pace and be directed at improving capabilities.

The reduced business base created by the survival actions will probably not be satisfactory for the long term. Thus, as performance improves, you need to press for new areas of growth and development. You hope that the costs of survival—in human, financial, and competitive terms—will not encumber your prospects for new opportunities.

Anticipatory Change

The impetus for anticipatory change comes from a sense that strategic change is needed, rather than from concrete evidence. As you size up the future of your business, you come to an unsettling conclusion that it is not prepared for a changing environment and that performance will suffer. The requirements for change are not particularly clear, however, and in part because of this uncertainty, you know it will be difficult to develop a general sense of urgency about the situation.

The early approach to anticipatory change will usually involve measured steps with selected, reasonably friendly key players. The pace will generally be quite slow, reflecting the need to develop an understanding of the situation before major commitments are made and to maintain flexibility as the action proceeds. The action focus will probably be quite narrow to start, but it will become much more complex as progress is made because the ultimate strategic shifts will usually encompass a wide-ranging set of objectives and a growing number of key players in the process. Leadership will likely be participative and dominated by careful, purposeful, incremental steps. This approach is generally referred to as *incrementalism.*[7]

The primary problem with incremental change is that it takes a lot of time and effort. It may take years to develop and put a major change in place. This is naturally distressing if you are an impatient manager, but a desire for fast action must be weighed against the benefits of a slower incremental approach.

Quinn argues that incrementalism is the most appropriate model for most strategic changes, because it helps executives to (1) improve the quality of information available; (2) deal with the different change objectives, key players, lead times, and sequencing problems involved in strategic change; (3) build the organizational awareness, understanding, and psychological commitment necessary for effective implementation; (4) overcome political and emotional barriers to change; and (5) improve the quality of their strategic analysis and choices by involving those people closest to the situation and by avoiding premature closure on the basis of potentially incorrect directions.[8]

One of the managers who participated heavily in the change process at Pepsi gave his view of the incremental process:

> It was hell, because we couldn't map out everything in advance. We didn't know what we were going to do tomorrow until we had lived it today. Finally, we realized, "We'll know as we go."[9]

Preliminary Work   The earliest item in anticipatory change is building your personal conviction that change is needed. There are two routes to pursue in this respect. The first is the standard strategic analysis that we have developed in this text—assessing the current strategy and concluding, as you move through the Diamond-E analysis, that future performance will not be satisfactory. This process, of course, will stimulate ideas about what is needed to bring the business back on course. It is the uncertainty surrounding your forecasts and conclusions that puts you in an anticipatory position.

The second route is to do the foregoing analysis backwards: build a vision of the business at some future point and then ask yourself whether the firm is likely to get there on its present course. Thus, you might ask what you would like the main characteristics of the business (scale, financial performance levels, strategic commitments, etc.) to be in five years, and whether your current strategy can achieve this. For Craig Weatherup at Pepsi, the vision was simple: achieve a 15 percent year-on-year annual increase in earnings, forever. The challenge was to make his management team agree that achieving that goal was feasible, and would require major changes in the way they did business.

Long-term visions can motivate and channel anticipatory change. There is a danger, though, that these visions may escape reality and become the product of fantasy and little else. There is always a need, as we pointed out in Chapter 2, for applying the Diamond-E drill to check for at least the vestiges of feasibility (remember, we are dealing with very uncertain conditions). Watch out, too, that your preliminary business definitions don't stimulate resistance from those who oppose that particular vision of the future. Both of these cautions support the idea of incrementalism, and of avoiding fixed destinations because they are risky to commit to in themselves and prone to spark resistance.

Target Groups   The first item on your agenda as you tackle anticipatory change is to identify your priority targets. You are looking for people who might be disposed to work on the situation with an open mind, who carry some weight in the organization, and with whom you have a reasonable relationship. You might face slim pickings in this regard, and the more difficult the situation, the more you should focus your choices. As stated earlier, Weatherup worked initially with his 10 direct reports, and he decided that the change initiative would not be rolled down to the next 70 managers in the organization until those 10 were fully on board. One of the managers recalled:

> We decided that we would not move forward until we were all aligned, until everyone supported it 100 percent. We would stop frequently for "alignment checks" to make sure that we had all contributed, we had all had the opportunity to be heard, and that we were all committed to support the decision. It consumed our lives . . . . By the time we were done, it was tattooed on our chests.[10]

First Steps There are an almost unlimited number of specific approaches that you can employ in taking an incremental approach to change. However, beneath the detail there are some common action principles, including the following:

1. Go beyond the formal processes of planning and control in the business to sense strategic needs and develop early awareness and understanding.

2. Develop preliminary diagnoses, and implement partial, directional solutions to strategic problems, rather than attempting to determine and implement a final correct strategy.

3. Incorporate feedback at all stages of the process to further clarify what is needed, to respond to opposition and to capitalize on support.

4. Build commitment over time as information develops, problems clarify, partial solutions prove their worth, and initial obstacles recede.

The major challenge in nearly all anticipatory change situations is creating commitment to the idea that change is required, while it is still unclear exactly what that change should be. Weatherup used the "burning platform" speech, borrowed from a consultant advising the company to create a sense of urgency.

> It seems that a few years ago a North sea oil rig caught fire. One worker, trained not to jump from the 150 foot high rig into the icy sea but to wait for help no matter how bad things got, leaped anyway. He survived. Asked afterward why he stepped off the edge, the worker said he looked behind him and saw an approaching wall of fire and looked down and saw the sea. "I chose probable death over certain death."[11]

Reactive Change

The impetus for reactive change comes from a tangible deterioration in business performance. If the deterioration is not reversed it will lead to critical difficulties. The situation combines elements of anticipatory and crisis change: it may be difficult to establish both the need and the appropriate direction for change, but the deterioration creates a sense of urgency, and a need to act without delay.

The early approach to reactive change will likely be to deal with two quite different internal target groups—those who support the changes and those who are creating bottlenecks in the process. The priority objectives in the first periods of work will be organization changes that will help the supporters of change focus on the needed strategic developments and, at the same time, help you to deal with the resistors. The leadership style will probably be a hybrid of a participative approach with those on board and a directive style with resistors.

Preliminary Work   Your first task as you prepare a plan for reactive change is to estimate the time that you have available. This is essentially a task of projecting the deterioration of the business and determining the point at which some form of crisis will thrust the business into chaos—a time-to-crisis calculation. This process will also be helpful in assessing the forces at work on the business and suggesting possible corrections. Remember that an established trend of deterioration tends to accelerate as competitors sense that you are vulnerable, and as good people leave because they see what is happening. The end may be closer than is first apparent.

Target Groups   Reactive changes usually call for you to work on two target groups more or less simultaneously: supporters and resistors. Given the time pressure it is critical that you identify and focus on the individuals or groups that are in a position to support or to resist the development and implementation of the required changes—what we call the *pivotal change targets*.

The pivotal change targets in many reactive change situations will be a cross-section of relatively senior managers. If these managers are capable and flexible, they will be a positive force in implementing change. If, on the other hand, some or all of these managers are poorly equipped to deal with change, they will constitute an extremely difficult obstacle. They have power, by virtue of their positions and the constituencies they represent, to cause real problems. They can, at least in the short run, dilute, deflect, and distort change initiatives from above and below.

Since individual managers in the pivotal groups have the potential to exercise great leverage on change, it is important to do a thorough job in assessing their readiness for change and in particular their ability to implement or resist the program. In this way, you can tailor your tactics to individuals. Harvey Golub, who took over as CEO of American Express in the early 1990s, when the company was well down the crisis curve, commented on his early meetings with his management team:

> *I was listening to reports, and although I had zero data, I did not believe what I was hearing. The way people talked didn't match what I thought was reality, although I could not point to particulars.*[12]

He began to assess the readiness of individuals for change based on

> *how people were describing things to me. People use phrases that indicate their readiness levels. You get a sense for whether they know what to do but are simply unwilling to act, don't know what to do, or understand what needs to be done but don't know how to do it.*[13]

Golub judged that readiness was low, and strong leadership was required. He commented: "You can quickly back off if your assessment turns out to be wrong. But most people find it punitive if you start by underleading and only later add structure."[14]

First Steps, Style, Pace   If the priority targets in the business are all ready to go, then you can focus on directly developing the new behaviours, capabilities, resources, and preferences that you need to implement your new strategy. More likely you will face a mixed situation of supporters and resistors, making it difficult to move so quickly. In this case, you need to help the willing get on with the job and spend at least some time encouraging the resistors to see the light. If they cannot change, you will have to move them out.

The most difficult decision you will have to make as you move through reactive change is whether the pace of change is consistent with the growing urgency of the situation. As we saw earlier, Jean-Pierre Rodier at Pechiney established a two-year time period in which major cost reductions would be achieved. Harvey Golub at American Express set a target of a $1-billion cost reduction in a three-year period. The problem facing managers in a reactive change setting is that the downward momentum of the business cannot usually be reversed immediately, and the deterioration of performance will likely continue for some time, regardless of the action being taken. This factor has two major consequences.

First, you will have to make tough judgments early in the process regarding the performance of individual members of the pivotal group. Are they aware of and responding to the situation? Is their action consistent with the urgency of the situation? Financial results may not yet show improvement, so close personal monitoring is essential. One of the first steps taken by Golub at American Express, for example, was to change the way managerial performance was assessed. Traditionally, a manager's performance had been assessed by comparing actual financial results against a budget. Golub changed that, judging performance against

> *what you should have done, given the circumstances. That reduces the manipulative component of the budget process and . . . by taking into account how the results were achieved, I made the criteria both more subjective and more objective at the same time. For example, if you meet your net income goals by cutting advertising expenses, you won't get a very high score.*[15]

Golub went further, recording his assessments in annual "report cards" that publicly graded managers on their performance in five categories: shareholders, customers, employees, re-engineering, and quality. Some managers liked the openness and clarity of this system; others did not. But it did change behaviour.

The second challenge that results from the fact that in reactive change situations "things are likely to get worse before they start to get better" is that opponents of the change program might seize upon the continuing performance deterioration and intensify their resistance. You do not have much time to accommodate such resistance and convert it to positive ends. You will have to deal with it aggressively. It is at this point that heads are most likely to roll.

The conclusion is that in reactive change situations you will probably be called on to use a mixture of directive and participative styles. The precise mix will vary with the support you have and the resistance you face. One general manager who had with mounting frustration debated with his senior management team for months as to whether or not change was required in their organization finally "drew a line in the sand" when he stated at the next meeting they would discuss only *what* changes should be made, not *if* change should be made. Those who did not feel that was an appropriate agenda were not required to attend. The impasse was broken, and planning for change proceeded in a participative fashion.

Creating an Action Plan

At this point you have established your guidelines for action, which means that you know your priority objectives, priority targets, first steps of action against each, your intended management style, and the necessary pace of change. The final step in the planning process is to detail the specific actions that follow logically from these general determinants. A format for this job is suggested in Figure 9.1. The first step is to decide on the time periods which are going to form the basis of your planning.

Time Periods   To get to specific action you need to break down the total time span that you think will be required for change into relatively short periods, such as the 90-day intervals that we discussed earlier. The most important of the periods is the first one, the second most important is the second one, and so on. The span of the early periods should reflect the urgency of the situation. In crisis it may be necessary to work in periods of a few days or perhaps a week at a time. There is more leeway in anticipatory and reactive change, but the maximum length allowed should be 90-day periods. If the periods are any longer, there is a tendency to get less specific about particular actions and timing.

Focus hard on the first period or two. Get them right and you are on your way. Get them wrong and you will be in big trouble. It is difficult to plan the later periods in any detail, anyway, because they will rely so much on what happens at the outset. The planning approach that is most useful for these later periods is to develop some basic contingency notions and then, as things unfold, to fill in the appropriate detailed actions.

Priority Objectives and Targets   This is where your identification of priority objectives and targets really counts. If the time period has been set correctly and you are realistic about what you can do, you will have a few focused objectives and targets on your first period list. In fact, if the list grows to more than a couple, you should reconsider your approach: your objectives may be insufficiently focused, or the time period that you have chosen to work with may be too long.

First Steps, Style, Timing   For each objective and key target you will specify precise early action steps. Taken together, these steps should achieve the objective for the period. There is usually no risk-free way forward, but do not hinge the first steps of your change program on miraculous changes in attitude or behaviour if you can avoid it. Your planned sequence of actions is likely to be important, as you may want to achieve success *vis-à-vis* some objectives and targets before you move to others. On the other hand, many managers find that they need to work on several change streams in parallel.

Avoid the temptation of trying to do too much, too quickly. A big stretch is a necessary risk in crisis, but it is usually avoidable elsewhere. If you choose objectives carefully and act with a clear focus, your change process will build on itself and reach its destination in a sure and timely fashion. The stories of failed change are stories of overly ambitious objectives and expansive action. Perhaps the most important ingredient in achieving successful strategic change is the personal discipline necessary to focus your thinking and your action.

SUMMARY

This chapter has outlined the required steps to move from the change objectives and starting conditions of a change program to a set of operational guidelines for action and thence to a detailed action plan.

The preparation of action guidelines in a specific situation is largely a matter of developing the implications of the change objectives and starting conditions (urgency, organizational readiness, and personal readiness) that were discussed in Chapter 9. It is useful to cast these implications in terms of three basic variable categories: (1) action priorities, which establish priority key players in the change process and objectives; (2) leadership style, which establishes the basic relationships and tactics to be used; and (3) pace, which establishes the required rate of change. Together these guidelines set up a definitive framework for specific actions.

The final step in the planning process is detailing the actions that follow logically from the guidelines. The major steps of this process are to (1) define a series of time periods; (2) indicate the key players that you wish to address within each time period; and (3) identify your priority objectives, tactics, and sequence of action within the time period.

NOTES

1. Peter Wall, *Canadian Business,* April 10, 1998, p. 35.

2. Robert H. Schaffer and Harvey A. Thomson, "Successful Change Programs Begin With Results," *Harvard Business Review* (January–February 1992), p. 80.

3. See for example: "Greg Brenneman: Right Away and All at Once: How We Saved Continental," *Harvard Business Review* (September–October 1998), p. 162.

4. Michael Beer, Russel A. Eisenstat, and Bert Spector, "Why Change Programs Don't Produce Change," *Harvard Business Review* (November–December 1990), p. 158.

5. James Weber and Michael Beer, Asda (A1), case 498-006. Boston: Harvard Business School, 1998, p. 2.

6. James Weber and Michael Beer, Asda (B), case 498-007. Boston: Harvard Business School, 1998, p. 16.

7. James Brian Quinn, *Strategies for Change: Logical Incrementalism* (Homewood, Illinois: Richard D. Irwin Inc., 1980).

8. ibid.

9. Don Sull and David A. Garvin, Pepsi's Regeneration, 1990–1993, case 395-048. Boston: Harvard Business School, 1996, p. 5.

10. ibid., pp. 3, 4.

11. Brain Dumaine, "Times are Good? Create a Crisis," *Fortune,* June 28, 1993, as reported in Don Sull and David A. Garvin, Pepsi's Regeneration, 1990–1993, case 395-048. Boston Harvard Business School, 1996. p. 4.

12. Artemis March and David A. Garvin, Harvey Golub: Recharging American Express, case 396-212. Boston: Harvard Business School, 1996, p. 7.

13. ibid., p. 7.

14. ibid., p. 7.

15. ibid., p. 7.

ADDITIONAL READINGS

AUGUSTINE, NORMAN A., "Managing the Crisis You Tried to Prevent," *Harvard Business Review* (November–December 1995), p. 147.

DUCK, JEANIE DANIEL, " Managing Change: The Art of Balancing," *Harvard Business Review* (November–December 1993), p. 109.

FREEDMAN, NIGEL, " Operation Centurion: Managing Transformation at Philips," *Long Range Planning*, vol. 29, no. 5, 1996, p. 607.

SADLER, PHILIP, *Managing Change*. London: Kogan Page, 1995.

STREBEL, PAUL, "Why Do Employees Resist Change?" *Harvard Business Review* (May–June 1996), p. 86.